DECODING THE WHY

HOW BEHAVIORAL SCIENCE
IS DRIVING THE NEXT GENERATION
OF PRODUCT DESIGN

NATE ANDORSKY

New Degree Press

Copyright © 2020 Nate Andorsky
All rights reserved.

DECODING THE WHY
How Behavioral Science is Driving the Next Generation of Product Design

ISBN 978-1-64137-550-4 *Paperback*
       978-1-64137-551-1 *Kindle Ebook*
       978-1-64137-552-8 *Digital Ebook*

*In loving memory of my grandfather Henry J. Walter,
from whom I continue to learn.*

*My grandfather believed that life is about discovering your
gift and finding a way to give it back to the world.*

*My hope is that his curiosity—for life, for how the world works, and
for how it all fits together—can be felt through the pages of this book.*

CONTENTS

INTRODUCTION: HOW TO USE THIS BOOK　　　　　　　7

PART I: THE NEW ERA OF PRODUCT DESIGN　　　　**13**
CHAPTER 1:　THE NEXT PRODUCT REVOLUTION WILL
　　　　　　　BE PSYCHOLOGICAL　　　　　　　　　15
CHAPTER 2:　HUMANS ARE COMPLICATED　　　　　33

PART II: MEETING OUR FUTURE SELVES　　　　　**39**
CHAPTER 3:　WHY WE FAIL TO MEET OUR FUTURE SELVES　41
CHAPTER 4:　IMAGINING YOUR FUTURE SELF　　　　51
CHAPTER 5:　DESIRE TO ACHIEVE　　　　　　　　　57
CHAPTER 6:　BRIDGING THE GAP BETWEEN INTENTION
　　　　　　　AND ACTION　　　　　　　　　　　　75
CHAPTER 7:　DON'T BREAK THE CHAIN　　　　　　87

PART III: BORN TO FOLLOW　　　　　　　　　　**97**
CHAPTER 8:　THE CUES WE TAKE FROM OTHERS　　　99
CHAPTER 9:　MANUFACTURING A SOCIAL NORM　　　105
CHAPTER 10: SIGNALS OF TRUST　　　　　　　　　115
CHAPTER 11: NEVER OUT OF THE GAME　　　　　　123

PART IV: HOW WE DECIDE　　　　　　　　　　　**135**
CHAPTER 12: DECISIONS, DECISIONS　　　　　　　137
CHAPTER 13: IT'S NOT WHAT YOU SAY,
　　　　　　　IT'S HOW YOU SAY IT　　　　　　　143
CHAPTER 14: SOMETHING TO LOSE　　　　　　　　153
CHAPTER 15: THE POWER OF PEANUTS AND DEFAULTS　167
CHAPTER 16: DRIVEN BY EMOTION　　　　　　　　177

PART V: THE FUTURE OF BEHAVIORAL SCIENCE   **195**

CHAPTER 17: THE FUTURE OF BEHAVIORAL SCIENCE   197

CHAPTER 18: INTEGRATING A BEHAVIORAL-FIRST APPROACH   205

ACKNOWLEDGMENTS   211

APPENDIX + FOOTNOTES   215

INTRODUCTION:

HOW TO USE THIS BOOK

Before starting your journey, review the suggestions below to help you get the most out of this book.

IDENTIFY WHAT YOU WANT OUT OF THIS BOOK
To get the most out of this book, first identify what you want out of the book and challenge yourself to find the answers as you read through the chapters. Ask yourself the questions below and determine where you fit in:

— Are you thinking of building a product and want to know how to build it with a behavioral-first approach?
— Have you created a product and are curious how to behaviorally optimize it?
— Are you interested in what drives human behavior?
— Are you an executive at a company with a product that has hit a growth plateau and are looking for new and innovative ways to spur growth?

— Are you involved in some capacity in product creation and looking to learn what the future of product design holds?

HOW THE BOOK IS BROKEN DOWN
The first chapter of each part provides an overview of what my company, Creative Science, calls "behavioral drivers." Before you can understand solutions to a problem, you must understand the cause of the problem. Each subsequent chapter in that section then focuses on one idea, "behavioral solution," to offset the behavioral driver. Think of the first chapter of each part as the problem we're trying to solve and each subsequent chapter as a proposed solution to help overcome said problem.

KEEP A PEN AND PAPER HANDY
As you consume the content in this book, you'll combine approaches from different chapters and dream up your own behavioral solutions. Be sure to jot these down. To test your ideas, refer to chapter 18 for instructions on how to do so.

UNDERSTAND THE BEHAVIOR AND THEN THE FEATURE
Understanding features built into a product is helpful, but without an understanding of why, much becomes lost in translation.

Grasping the psychological underpinnings of why a feature was built is where the learning happens. This understanding allows you to understand the psychology under the hood, enabling you to extrapolate and apply psychological concepts in various contexts.

Without this understanding, you fall into the bad habit of duplicating innovative features with no rationale for doing so.

You see a feature that works in one context, copy and paste it wherever you'd like, and then wonder why you don't see the same effectiveness.

TERMS YOU MAY NOT BE FAMILIAR WITH

If you work in the technology space, you'll be familiar with the terms below. However, if you are unfamiliar with product design, I've defined commonly used words in this book for your reference below:

- **Product**–a consumer-facing software product or website. A product could be a mobile app, a web application, or a website. Some examples are Acorns, Airbnb, Facebook, Twitter, etc.
- **Product Design**–the look, feel, and experience of a product (referenced above), which could range from aesthetics to choices a designer has made for how a user navigates through a product.
- **User Experience**–the experience a user has when using a product such as what they may be feeling or thinking, or how hard or easy the product is to use.
- **Intervention**–refers to a change made to a product to test the effectiveness of a behavioral science theory. For example, to show a user how much money they were spending daily, the behavioral scientist created a graph that the user would see when using the app. In this case, the intervention is the graph. Intervention is a fancy term for a change.
- **User**–anyone who uses a product as defined above.

CONTEXT MATTERS

The examples in this book provide insight into how various theories integrate into product design. The application of these theories may seem obvious after the fact, but the road that led to those conclusions was often not. Behind every successful application of behavioral science, substantial testing of multiple approaches failed before discovering a strategy that worked.

This book is intended to give you a baseline understanding of how behavioral science integrates into product design. Still, please know that to grasp the material, you'll need to put these ideas into practice.

The field of study is contextual, and small changes to an environment can change the effect of a theory or an approach. Behavioral science and its applications are not one size fits all. Simply because a theory works well in this book does not mean it will work the same way when leveraged in your product. However, this should not discourage you from integrating what you learn in this book. I cannot stress enough that it is essential to TEST. TEST. TEST. Do not assume that because a strategy learned in this book worked, it will work in your specific use case.

JUST GET STARTED

Go ahead and dig in. Start anywhere. Well, just not at the end. The best way to learn this material is to get your hands dirty. Take these concepts and implement them today.

It is okay to jump around.

Even though most of the chapters reference products and theories from previous chapters, each chapter can stand on its own. However, if you do jump around, I recommend reading chapter 1, as it provides a foundation for everything shared in the book. Without this foundation, you may get lost.

SHARE THIS BOOK

Give it to friends, siblings, mothers, brothers, aunts, dogs, cats, or even a gerbil. I am passionate about behavioral science, and I am a true believer that this is the next generation of product design. The more people are exposed to this approach, the better. Set a goal to lend it to at least one friend after you finish it.

REACH OUT

I am an open book and love to chat about behavioral science and technology. To connect with me, feel free to ping me on LinkedIn (search Nate Andorsky), email me at nate@creativescience.co, or visit my company's website at www.creativescience.co.

PART I:
THE NEW ERA OF PRODUCT DESIGN

CHAPTER 1:

THE NEXT PRODUCT REVOLUTION WILL BE PSYCHOLOGICAL

Imagine you're the CEO of a homeowners and renters insurance company. You've just left the annual board meeting with marching orders: reduce fraudulent claims by 50 percent, or find a new job come next year. The board is concerned; fraudulent claims are costing the company millions of dollars every year. To drastically reduce fraudulent claims, they're suggesting an overhaul of the company's fraud department.

Leaving the meeting, your head is spinning. You are cycling through ways to attack this problem. Worried about losing your job, you ask trusted peers to lend their advice.

What do you do? What is your strategy to reduce fraudulent claims? I've asked this question to friends, family, and colleagues, and I've received a myriad of responses.

"First, I'd review our overall claims process. I'd assume part of the reason claims are so high could be due to poor investigations of claims. I'd ensure we were adequately staffed to investigate each claim thoroughly and we're asking the right questions during the claims process. I'd also do a technology audit to ensure the technology we are using is helping us to identify and flag potentially fraudulent claims," said my friend Carl.

"I'd review our claims process and identify the demographic information as it relates to the customers filing fraudulent claims. I'd look to create personas based on the types of people who typically file fraudulent claims. This would help us flag future potential fraudulent claims," said another one of my friends Charlotte.

Try it, ask a friend this question and they'll probably say something similar.

They'll decide to create or enhance the fraud department by staffing it with people to conduct interviews to ensure claims were legitimate. If your friend is somewhat sophisticated, he or she may even propose developing a machine learning algorithm that would help identify potential fraudulent claims. The algorithm would understand the characteristics and patterns of previous fraudulent claims and then use this data to flag new claims as potentially fraudulent before handing them off to a team member for follow-up.

Most companies attempt to fix the surface-level problems, but there is a fundamental flaw with this approach. It fails to consider the underlying behaviors driving the problem. Rather, this solution immediately jumps to create guard rails and systems to prevent the problem from persisting. It is not that their approach wouldn't work, but it only addresses only part of the equation.

The board tasked you with reducing fraudulent claims, but that's not the problem that needs to be fixed. The real challenge lies in trust, or the lack thereof.

Fraudulent claims are a byproduct of a broken system of trust. This lack of trust contributes to insurance companies needing to create expensive systems of checks and balances to counter mistrust. Think about it. If all customers were trustworthy, no fraudulent claims would exist; the systems that identify fraudulent claims would no longer serve a purpose.

If the issue is a broken system of trust, your goal is to increase trust, not decrease fraudulent claims. This approach reduces fraudulent claims, a byproduct of solving the problem of trust. With this new goal in mind, now how do you rethink the problem from a *behavioral-first* approach?

I borrowed the insurance hypothetical from a real-life example.

Meet the new insurance company: Lemonade.

Lemonade is a fast-growing insurance app offering renters and home insurance powered by tech and driven by social good. The product is a beautiful blend of behavioral science and AI and is taking the insurance industry by storm. They've taken a unique, behavioral-first approach to building their business down to reducing fraudulent claims.[1]

Their Chief Behavioral Science Officer is the infamous Dan Ariely. He is the James B. Duke Professor of Psychology and Behavioral Economics at Duke University, and a founding member of the Center for Advanced Hindsight. He is the author of numerous books, including *Predictably Irrational* and *The Upside of Irrationality*, and viewers have seen his *TED* talks over fifteen million times.[2]

---

1. "Lemonade: Forget Everything You Know About Insurance."
2. Dan Ariely, "All About Dan."

Lemonade approaches this problem from a *behavioral-first* angle by analyzing the social, cognitive, and emotional factors that could help build a stronger system of trust. They asked themselves, how do you design a system of trust?

In a recent *TED* talk, Dan noted, "Let's change it from a two-player game to a three-player game. How does this help? When you join Lemonade, you pick a charity you love. Every month, Lemonade takes a fixed amount as profit, pays back claims, and if there is money left over in the pool, a portion of it goes to the charity you selected. Now, it's a game between you and the charity. Now, if you cheat the system, you are no longer cheating your insurance company, you're cheating your favorite charity."[3]

They didn't stop there. When a customer submits a claim, part of filing a claim requires the customer to record a video of themselves reporting the claim. Lemonade knows that people are less likely to lie on video than on a written form. In the step before a customer submits a claim, Lemonade asks the customer to sign an honesty pledge. This pledge shows the customer's face at the time of signing and has the following statement:

"Pledge of Honesty—I pledge that I am part of a community of people who trust each other to be honest. I promise to claim only what I deserve."[4]

This honestly pledge step reminds the user about the type of person they aspire to be. The term "community"

---

[3] Dan Ariely, "Designing for Trust."
[4] Jeanne Bliss, "Lemonade Insurance: Powering Rapid Growth Through Radical Transparency and Technology."

here leverages the concept that the customer is part of a broader community who are all in this together, urging them to not break the "circle of trust" and let the community down.[5]

Lemonade asks the customer to sign and then click a button that reads, "I swear I'll be honest."

Dan closes his *TED* talk by recounting an email he received from a customer, "I told you somebody stole my laptop, but it turns out I actually just misplaced it. How do I return the money?" Dan was baffled. He wasn't sure what to do. He called a few of his colleagues in the insurance industry to ask how to handle such a scenario. None of them knew as this had never happened before.

"If you create a system that creates trust, and you trust people, trust will come back," said Dan as he closes out his *TED* talk.[6]

We walk around with computers in our pockets that are more powerful than the computer systems that sent the first spaceship to the moon.[7] In 2015, the International Telecommunication Union estimated that about 3.2 billion people, almost half of the world's population, would be online by the end of the year.[8] Average mobile usage (which includes

---

5   Ainsley Harris, "Lemonade Is Using Behavioral Science to Onboard Customers and Keep Them Honest."
6   Dan Ariely, "Designing for Trust."
7   Tibi Puiu, "Your smartphone is millions of times more powerful than all of NASA's combined computing in 1969."
8   "Internet used by 3.2 billion people in 2015."

both smartphones and tablets) has increased from 0.3 hours per day in 2008 to 3.3 hours a day in 2017.[9]

Intertwined in every facet of our lives, technology lives at the focal point of many of our decisions. An alarm clock on our phone awakens us, and we fall asleep asking Alexa to fill us in on the day's news. Our days begin and end with technology. Whether it's the phone in your pocket, the computer you work on, the cash register you pay on, or the Uber you summoned to take you to work, it is difficult to recall a time when twenty-four hours passed in the absence of an interaction with technology.

Whether it is a website, a mobile app, or an online application, screens live at the intersection of many of our choices. Consequently, these screens have the power to influence how or what we decide and, if handled correctly, these screens can help us make better decisions.

We are entering a new frontier—one where implementing a behavioral-first approach will be where companies gain an edge on their competition. There are hundreds of fitness apps on the market. Yours may look great and have all the features users want, but that won't set it apart from your competition. Gone are the days when all you needed was a great idea and a beautifully designed product. Those are a dime a dozen now, and users yearn for more.

It was the summer of 2017, and a friend of mine recommended a book titled *Nudge* by Richard Thaler and Cass Sunstein. As

---

[9] Rob Marvin, "Tech Addiction by the Numbers: How Much Time We Spend Online."

I dug in, I began to learn about behavioral science, a field of study that uncovers the social, cognitive, and emotional factors impacting our decision-making. I was fascinated by how much of our decision-making happens outside of our conscious awareness.[10]

I was in awe of Thaler and Sunstein's work as they referenced study after study, all of which illustrate the internal and external factors that nudge people to act. Some actions we believe are within our control, but the evidence suggests otherwise. Spending nearly a decade helping companies build software products, I was familiar with several high-level concepts from *Nudge*. For example, leveraging social proof in the form of testimonials: If other people say your product is quality, it increases the likelihood a prospective buyer will purchase your product.

However, I quickly learned that I was merely scratching the surface. Decades of research existed with the sole goal of figuring out what drives human behavior. This research extended beyond placing testimonials on a website and calling it "social proof." This research understood the fundamental building blocks that explain why we do what we do.

As I dug into the research, I learned that 95 percent of our thoughts, emotions, and learning happen before we are consciously aware of them.[11] However, much of today's technology is built on the other 5 percent—the part users can articulate when they're in focus groups, when they're filling out surveys, or when they're providing feedback to builders about what they think the next version of the product or

---

10 Richard H. Thaler and Cass R. Sunstein, *Nudge: Improving Decisions about Health, Wealth, and Happiness*.
11 Gerald Zaltman, *How Customers Think: Essential Insights into the Mind of the Market*.

website should be. The stories users tell us are often post rationalizations of their decisions. They did y because of x. If you want them to do more of y, put more of x into your technology. You do what your users ask, but you find yourself running in circles.

"The way we typically build technology and run startups reflects the way we do everything else in society: ask people what they need and give it to them. Or better yet, take a guess about what people need, and then use our intuition to build the thing we think they need," said Julie O'Brien, Director of Behavior Change at WW (formerly Weight Watchers).

It's not that users are intentionally lying to you. Much of our decision-making happens outside of our conscious awareness. Most of the time, you're asking users to provide explanations of behaviors they don't truly understand themselves.

"When you do this, it leads to building products that underperform because they don't account for how humans make decisions. Rather, they are built around our assumptions and what users tell us, but users don't know what they want," she added.

As numerous studies prove, Julie's theory isn't just an opinion. In the 1960s, several researchers conducted an experiment that won them the Nobel prize. They took split-brain patients, patients in which the left half and the right half of the brain had been disconnected. Split-brain surgery, or corpus callosotomy, is a drastic way of alleviating epileptic seizures. The procedure involves severing the corpus callosum, the primary bond between the brain's left and right hemispheres."[12]

---

12   Berit Brogaard, "Split Brains."

The left side and right side of your brain each control half of your body. The researchers would talk to one side of the brain and tell it to do something, and then ask the other side of the brain why the action was taken. For example, the researchers may instruct one side of the brain to stand up. The patient stands up, and then the researcher would ask the other side of the patient's brain why the action was taken. The honest answer would be, "I don't know," as the two sides of the brain are disconnected, so one side of the brain couldn't hear what the other side of the brain was saying.

But that's not what happened; patients consistently had a confident explanation. If you asked them why they stood up, they would say something such as, "I was going to grab some food to eat." When we don't know why we took an action, we make up an explanation.[13]

What if we don't know why we do what we do? What if we can't articulate or realize our true motivations for using products or services or making a specific decision? What if even when we think we know why we did something, we're wrong?[14]

When it comes to explaining our decision-making process, we are wrong a lot more than we realize. We act and create a narrative that matches our identity to justify the action we took, but we're only aware of a small part of the picture driving our decisions.

"The challenge is that you can't get reliable information out of people by asking them directly, so relying on user

---

13   Lukas J. Volz and Michael S. Gazzaniga, "Interaction in isolation: 50 years of insights from split-brain research. 2051-2060.
14   Kevin Simler and Robin Hanson. *The Elephant in the Brain: Hidden Motives in Everyday Life.*

feedback or your assumptions about user feedback is never going to tell you the full story, and this has led to a huge amount of waste in product design." Julie added.

As seen in the split-brain study, we often don't know why we make certain decisions. There are factors at play, both internally and externally, influencing every decision we make that we aren't consciously aware of. Because of this, when we build technology, we look to solve the obvious issue that our users tell us, which narrows our thinking and prevents us from asking questions about what other underlying behaviors could be driving the problem.

Through my research, I quickly found some companies were optimizing products. They were trying various layouts, colors, etc., A/B testing approaches, and then optimizing. They tried many ideas until one worked—move a button here, change a color here, lay these elements out this way. If they arrived at a strategy that worked, they often didn't know why, and this meant they couldn't extrapolate it to solve other problems. Few companies were taking a behavioral-first approach, such as the one Lemonade did.

In "Imagining the Next Decade of Behavioral Science," Evan Nesterak has seen this too. "…it is surprising to discover how little research in human behavior normally goes in their design."[15]

Their best approach was to research competitors in their space, analyze their products, and then create variations of a design concept based on what their competitors were doing. They reasoned that if a competitor's company was successful, their product must be optimized and rooted in science. Mimicking competitors' products creates an echo-chamber

---

15   Evan Nesterak, "Imagining the Next Decade of Behavioral Science."

of product design. Everyone starts doing what everyone else is doing with little to no evidence that it works.

Technology has driven progress for decades, and industries have reacted accordingly by dedicating enormous amounts of time and resources to progress in this domain by building bigger, faster, and more sophisticated systems. But what if the key to unlock the potential of your venture is not simply faster, better technology, but rather an understanding of what drives human behavior?

Matt Wallaert, author of *Start at the End*, notes that even though we have upward of forty years of robust foundational research, the academic knowledge precedes implementation by about fifteen years. There is a considerable amount of economic potential to be released by integrating a behavioral-first approach to product design.

If several software engineers are analyzing a problem, they're most likely going to solve it with an engineering solution. But if you have individuals with psychology and behavioral backgrounds, they'll view it through a different lens. It reframes the question, which reframes the potential answers.

As Rory Sutherland, Executive Creative Director of Ogilvy and author of *Alchemy*, notes, "We didn't have a framework for psychological problems before Daniel Kahneman. For too long, we've put too much weight on solving technological problems, but not psychological problems."

Rory believes the next revolution won't be technological. It will be psychological. Although scientific interest in psychology surfaced around the mid-nineteenth century, we have only recently begun to develop frameworks for applying it in everyday decision-making. With this framework came the rise of behavioral economics, which falls under the broad term of behavioral science, which provides a road map for understanding, predicting, and influencing human behavior. [16,17]

Tim Ogilvie, the founder of the design thinking firm Peer Insight, refers to the two types of data that many forward-thinking companies collect as SAY and DO data.

SAY data is the subjective information collected from users. SAY data comes in the form of user interviews, focus groups, surveys, workshops—any type of information users relay to your team. SAY data is what your users verbally tell you, providing reasons for why they did something, or why they will do something in the future. Product roadmaps are typically built based on this by asking users what they want and then giving it to them. However, the SAY data is often wrong, misleading, or only tells a small part of the story.

DO data are the analytics—what users are doing on your website or product. DO data is gathered through tracking software such as Google Analytics, heat-mapping, or a custom tracking tool.

Companies incorporate SAY and DO data into their product strategy and roadmap. They take in user surveys and feedback and collect various data points on their product's performance.

We're inept at relaying what drives our past behaviors and predicting what we'll do in future situations. Product owners often see this too. SAY data doesn't match the DO

---

16 Rory Sutherland, "The Next Revolution Will Be Psychological, Not Technological."
17 Rory Sutherland, "Perspective is Everything."

data. Users tell them one thing (SAY data) but do (DO data) something completely different.

This book uncovers the third piece—the WHY data. If you understand the WHY data behind the DO and SAY data, it unlocks a world of possibilities. With the WHY data, you can build products with a behavioral-first approach. You know the behaviors driving your users' decisions, rather than following their surface-level sentiments.

What users do is more important than what users tell us, and it's our job to dig into academic research and understand *why* users do what they do. Users don't know what they want, and it's our job to figure it out, not by asking them, but by understanding them. Of course, we should listen to what users tell us, but we should take it with a grain, actually mounds, of salt.

We shouldn't rely on what our intuition tells us, nor what our users tell us, but what the decades of research about human behavior tell us. We should be incorporating theories about human behavior into product design and letting the data tell us the real story. We need to move forward with a deep understanding of what drives human behavior, bridge the gap between theory and practice, and rigorously test those approaches to uncover the behavioral truth.

As the CEO of Creative Science, a digital agency that uses behavioral science to build digital strategies and technology for today's most innovative companies, I've spent over a decade working with all types of organizations. They range from nonprofits and venture capital firms to start-ups and well-established Fortune 500 companies. I've been fortunate to do work on behalf of the Leonardo DiCaprio Foundation as well as Steve and Jean Case. I helped build an

Ebola Tracker for the ONE Campaign, and I created digital campaigns for the World Wildlife Fund.

I've had the opportunity to learn from the best in the field, such as academics from Harvard Business School, University of Pennsylvania, and the University of Virginia. I was certain that builders were integrating behavioral science into product design; yet, the more I dug, the more I realized I was wrong—most of the brilliant research remains in academia.

I found through my book research that individuals building products with a behavioral-first approach are getting better results because they are doing things differently. They have the DO and the SAY data, but most importantly, they've decoded the WHY data.

They know what questions to ask. They do not waste time because they start with an understanding of human behavior. They ask questions that address the root of the problem, not what users tell them. This enables them to come up with ideas others had never thought of. Just like Lemonade, without an understanding of trust, you would have never thought to ask users to submit their claims via video or to integrate a charitable giving aspect into the claims process. Your focus would have been on what your users were telling you and, therefore, the solution you built would be based on that SAY data.

The creators who build products with a behavioral-first approach dig into the academic research and understand the subconscious factors that influence human decision-making. Then, they use these theories as a foundation to develop and test various approaches to product design.

Their "behavioral design" is not randomly tweaking layouts, colors, and buttons to see how conversions and engagement metrics improve. Rather, they go a layer deeper and understand the psychology behind human decision-making—the external and internal factors that influence our decision process.

When you find the behavioral truth and understand the WHY, your view of product design shifts. You begin asking different questions you would have never thought of previously. With different questions, you develop different hypotheses, and with different hypotheses, you develop unconventional solutions. When you've found the WHY, you never start from scratch, and you have evidence to back up intuition. This foundation of informed assumptions cuts out backtracking, guessing, and headaches while driving concept ideation, creation, and testing.

It expands your horizons and provides you with a framework upon which to dream up brand new, outside-of-the-box concepts. Built on an understanding of human behavior, these concepts have a higher likelihood of success.

While context plays a significant role in how our behavior manifests, the underlying mechanisms remain constant. You can use the WHY data to extrapolate insights to tackle additional challenges. Even if you run into unprecedented problems later, you can refer back to the same understanding of human behavior to find clues to identify the mechanism driving those behaviors.

Through my research writing this book, I could not help but wonder—how many of us are missing the larger picture?

How many of us are designing and building products, but only understanding a small fraction of what drives user behavior? How many of us are missing golden opportunities hidden in plain sight because we don't know what drives human behavior but rather we build based on our intuition?

Nathaniel Barr, a professor of creativity and creative thinking at Sheridan College and a scientific advisor at

BEworks, notes, "The future of behavioral science will, and must, be more creative and more technologically advanced to rise to the challenges that await."[18]

At Creative Science, we believe an untapped opportunity lies in the fusion of technological innovation and psychological insights.

If we unleash this opportunity, could the software that helps individuals lose weight, exercise more, save money, or learn a new skill have a greater impact? And given that these apps touch millions upon millions of people daily, could integrating a behavioral-first approach to building technology have wide-reaching social impact? My team at Creative Science believes so.

To realize the true potential of what we build, we believe technological innovation must blend with an understanding of human psychology. To develop technology that lives up to its potential, we must understand the social, cognitive, and emotional factors that influence our decision-making process. Not what we think or what our intuition tells us, but rather what the science tells us about why we do what we do. Then, we must rigorously split test these science-backed approaches until the data shows us what is working. Our innovations will only live up to their full potential if they are built on an understanding of the human experience.

We need to start building with a behavioral-first approach.

If you're an entrepreneur, product manager, developer, or designer who is wondering how you can increase user

---

[18] Evan Nesterak, "Imagining the Next Decade of Behavioral Science."

conversions, retention, and engagement, this book is for you. If you're wondering how to get an edge on your competition, this book is for you. If you're wondering how you can better meet your users where they are, this book is for you. If you're on the road to product-market fit or have just found product-market fit but can't quite figure out how to get hockey-stick growth, this book is for you. If you're looking for a place where you can come up with new product ideas and need a foundation upon which to do so, this book is for you.

If you oversee strategy or revenue generation and you are looking to gain an edge over your competition by increasing conversions, engagement, and retention, this book is for you. Or maybe you're just fascinated with human behavior and how that can drive product design. This book is for you.

Decoding the Why is not technical jargon and broad theory without application and actionable insights. You won't walk away saying, "Well, now I know a lot about human behavior, but I have no idea how to implement it into product design."

On our journey through this book, we'll bridge the gap between theory and practice by showing you how the most innovative companies start with an understanding of human behavior to build successful products that see an increase in conversions, engagement, and retention rates because they tap into our human side.

I'll be walking you through the approach, the underlying behavioral theories that drive product decisions, and the strategies for implementation that allow these companies to build products on an understanding of the human experience. I'll be showing you the science behind why specific theories work, uplifting decades of research that explain why, how, and when to use them in your product design. With this knowledge, you'll be able to dream up new product features because you'll understand the psychological factors at play rather than just building a feature because it sounds exciting.

Toward the end of the book, I'll show you tactical steps for how to build, test, and optimize your products on a foundation of human behavior. I'll walk you through the steps of building behavioral-first products by showing you how we identify symptoms, map those to behavioral drivers, map those to behavioral solutions, create concepts and interventions based on our findings, and then test their effectiveness. And finally, I'll lay out what I think is next for the behavioral science field in the coming decade and how you can ride the next wave and begin decoding the WHY.

CHAPTER 2:

HUMANS ARE COMPLICATED

The year was 1942, and Daniel Kahneman was a young boy living in German-occupied Paris. Years prior, the Nazis had risen to power and were imprisoning and exterminating Jews by the millions. As a Jew himself, Daniel feared for his life. The Nazis required Daniel to wear a Jewish star in public at all times, identifying him to any passerby as a member of what the Nazis considered to be an inferior race.

One evening, Daniel was out past curfew, roaming the streets of Paris. To hide his identity, he turned his sweater inside out concealing the Jewish star sewn into the fabric. Strolling down the street, an SS officer spotted Daniel, noticing he had broken curfew. The officer summoned Daniel over to him. As Daniel approached the officer, he trembled with terror, fearful of what was about to happen to him and certain this officer would arrest him and his fate would become the fate of so many Jews before him.

With Daniel's heart pounding, hands trembling with fear, he slowly stepped toward the officer. This event would forever change the way Daniel viewed the world and the people who occupy it.

The officer picked Daniel up and hugged him tightly. He then opened his wallet and showed him a wrinkled black and white photo of a little boy. He gave Daniel some money, and the two went their separate ways, never to see each other again.

"Obviously, I reminded him of his son, and he, you know, he wanted to hug his son, so he hugged me," said Daniel.

"The complexity was that it's the combination of somebody who must have done some very evil things and had thought some very evil thoughts and yet, he was hugging me," he added.[19]

Humans are complicated. The intricacies of what drives our behavior are often hidden deep beneath the surface. In certain contexts, in certain environments, and around certain people, we may do one thing. But change any of those variables, and the corresponding actions and outcomes may change.

This experience followed Daniel for the rest of his life and served as the foundation for him to try to understand what makes humans so complex. Daniel Kahneman and his good friend Amos Tversky would grow up to become some of the most influential figures in understanding what drives human behavior. In search of answers, they began to challenge standard economic theory. They wondered if other factors that weren't purely economic influenced our behavior.

Standard economic theory rests on one simple yet powerful idea—humans are rational. We seek out the best information, carefully weigh the costs and benefits of our actions, and then maximize our gains and minimize our losses.[20]

---

19 Shankar Vedantam, et al, "Daniel Kahneman on Misery, Memory, and Our Understanding of the Mind."
20 Sendhil Mullainathan and Richard H. Thaler, "Behavioral Economics."

This idea has been around for centuries. Government policies, advocacy campaigns, and marketing tactics, among other things, have been formulated based on this approach. If you provide people with the economic costs and benefits of a potential decision, they'll select the optimal choice. If you want people to choose one option over the other, ensure the benefits outweigh the costs.

About fifty years ago, this way of thinking began to change.

"Behaviors don't necessarily reflect personality, but they have a lot to do with the situation. So, if people behave in strange ways, look at the situation they are in and the pressures that make them this way," added Daniel.[21]

Amos Tversky and Daniel Kahneman questioned this core fundamental belief that standard economic theory rested upon. They started asking, "What if we aren't as rational as we think?" They spent hours together talking, coming up with playful thought experiments about how and why humans would act differently depending on the situation, and then testing those hypotheses. Before long, they began to understand that human behavior often runs contrary to what standard economics would predict.[22]

Heather Graci, a Behavioral Economics Specialist at Creative Science, considers, "What if we feel things that aren't economic? The idea that emotion lies outside the realm of rational decision-making assumes that it has no value. The experience of emotion, positive or negative, is just as much an economic incentive as money, time, or other tangible resources."

---

21 Shane Parrish and Daniel Kahneman, "Daniel Kahneman: Putting Your Intuition on Ice."
22 Daniel Kahneman, *Thinking, Fast and Slow*.

Tversky and Kahneman's insights transformed the way we understand the human decision-making process, how factors that aren't purely economic can influence our decision-making. Their seminal paper, "Judgment Under Uncertainty: Heuristics and Biases," proposed that we attack complex problems using a limited number of heuristic principles—basically shortcuts.[23]

Our brain cannot consciously process every decision we have to make, so we take shortcuts to conserve brainpower. These shortcuts rely on internal and external cues, many of which we're not consciously aware of. Think about the simple task of walking. Walking is an action you take without ever thinking about it. Imagine if you had to instruct your body to complete every single task involved in walking. Walking would be nearly impossible. If you did manage to do it, you'd look like a child learning to walk for the first time, and you wouldn't have the time or brainpower to accomplish much else.

In Daniel Kahneman's book, *Thinking, Fast and Slow*, he proposes that the brain typically operates in one of two modes: automatic and reflective, often referred to as System 1 and System 2 thinking.

System 1 runs on autopilot. It's responsible for the types of decisions we often don't think about. When someone throws a ball at your head, you duck. You don't look at the ball, calculate the ball's speed, determine the likelihood that it will strike your face, and then make a decision to duck. It's reflexive, and it happens without conscious thought. This system is fast, and while it's often quite reliable, it can also be

---

23 Amos Tversky and Daniel Kahneman, "Judgment under uncertainty: Heuristics and biases." 1124-1131.

error-prone. These errors in judgment have long been written off as anomalies, but behavioral economics has found that these errors in judgment are systematic and, therefore, predictable.

System 2 is slower, more methodical, and dedicated to solving complex problems. Think about tackling a challenging math problem, organizing a trip for your friends, or debating the ends of the universe. System 2 is typically quite reliable but slow. Often, actions will start in System 2 and move over to System 1 as your brain begins to create habit loops.[24]

I grew up playing the piano. One of the first pieces I ever learned was "The Entertainer." For months, my mom and dad would have to listen as I pecked away slowly at the piano, often striking incorrect keys and taking upward of thirty minutes to make it through a single piece of music. Within a few months, after hours and hours of practicing, I could play the piece from start to finish in a few minutes without even thinking about it. My brain was on autopilot. Learning to play the piano is a prime example of a skill moving from System 2 to System 1.

Behavioral economics helps explain why seemingly random information can impact how we answer questions. Try grabbing a bunch of friends and finding a wheel with numbers from zero to one hundred on it. One by one, ask each friend to spin the wheel and then ask each one to estimate the number of African nations in the UN. You'll quickly find that their answers seem to be influenced by the number randomly shown on the wheel (the "anchor"). If the number displayed on the wheel is high, their answer is high; if the

---

24 Daniel Kahneman, *Thinking, Fast and Slow.*

number is low, their response is low. Your friend knows that pure chance generates the number on the wheel and is no way related to the question, yet it still impacts their guess.

It also helps to explain why we're risk-averse in seeking gains. Why most people, if given the option of a 100 percent chance of winning $10 or a 90 percent chance of winning $20, will take the first option. The expected payout of the second option is greater at $18 (90% x $20 = $18) compared to $10, but we cherish certainty. We'd rather opt for what is certain, the $10 option, than what is uncertain, even if the uncertain payout is higher.[25,26]

Throughout this book, we'll dig into the theories and take you on a journey through the human mind to understand the social, cognitive, and emotional factors at play when we make decisions. We'll understand why simply giving users rational reasons to act doesn't work. Then, we'll tie it into what this means for designing products to help users achieve better versions of themselves—whether that's saving more money, eating healthier, working out more, learning a new skill, or other positive goals. Let's get going.

---

25   Amos Tversky and Daniel Kahneman, "Prospect theory: An analysis of decision under risk." 263-291.
26   Daniel Kahneman, *Thinking, Fast and Slow*.

PART II:
MEETING OUR FUTURE SELVES

CHAPTER 3:

WHY WE FAIL TO MEET OUR FUTURE SELVES

"And the winner is Matthew McConaughey!" It was the 2014 Oscars, and Jennifer Lawrence had just announced that Matthew McConaughey had won best actor for his performance in *Dallas Buyers Club*. As the crowd rose to their feet in applause, McConaughey stood up, kissed his wife, and hugged Leonardo DiCaprio as he made his way to the stage. As he accepted his Oscar, the crowd quieted their applause and took their seats in anticipation of McConaughey's speech.

He proceeded to thank the people who had been instrumental in helping him achieve this momentous milestone, such as his family, his friends, his film and production crew, and even the other contestants. After a heartfelt speech, he ended with a moving anecdote.

"When I was fifteen years old, I had a very important person in my life come to me and say, 'Who's your hero?' I said, 'I don't know, I gotta think about that, give me a couple of weeks.'

This person comes back two weeks later and says, 'Who's your hero?'

I replied, 'You know what, I thought about it, you know who it is? It's me in ten years.'

So I turn twenty-five. Ten years later, that same person comes to me and says, 'So are you a hero?'

I replied, 'No, no, no, not even close.'

'Why?' she said.

'Cause my hero is me at thirty-five,' I said.

See, every day, every week, every month, every year of my life, my hero is always ten years away. I'm never going to meet my hero, I am never going to obtain that, and that's totally fine because it gives me somebody to keep on chasing."[27]

McConaughey's message is profound and the underlying theme speaks to an idea to which we can all relate—how fleeting our future selves can be. The new skill you want to learn, the weight you want to lose, the money you want to save—your goals are well-intentioned, but your actions don't always match up. Studies show that if you eat healthier and exercise regularly, you are more likely to live longer. Time is precious. It's the one thing we can't get back, yet we don't follow doctors' orders. Rationally, we know we should engage in positive behaviors. Still, too often, we fall short, and when we do, we seek to correct our actions by providing ourselves with rational reasons to achieve the goals we just failed to complete.

After all, if people were rational in this regard, providing them reasons to do so would be working, but it's not. It is not that we don't believe the data, but we are seldom motivated by

---

27   Oscars, "Matthew McConaughey winning Best Actor."

the data. We don't dispute that exercising and eating better is a wise decision, but we often fail to follow through on our intentions, a pattern you'll see at the turn of every year.

It's January 1, 2020, and I've just walked into my local YMCA. 2019 has come to a close, and with a new year comes new aspirations and a willingness to improve. I, along with millions of others, have set new goals for the new year. We all want to become better versions of ourselves, and we are all at the YMCA to start becoming that person.

As I pass the front desk person, I get the friendly, "Hello, Happy New Year!" I scan my membership card and walk past entrance into a large room with various types of workout equipment—from weight machines to treadmills—but this day seems a bit different than most days.

"Ugh, man," I complain to myself under my breath. I should have known better. Of course, everyone made a New Year's Resolution to go to the gym, and I shouldn't be surprised that the gym is this packed. I walk right by the weights and over to the locker room to get changed for the lap pool, but every lane has at least two people in it.

For the next thirty days, I notice the gym gradually empties. Every day, I arrive at approximately the same time, but every day, fewer people are there. By the time the end of February rolls around, the gym is back to normal attendance levels.

So often, we set goals to become better versions of ourselves, yet too often, we fail to achieve those. We blame it on external and internal factors, putting off what we should do today until tomorrow. Our ambition to reach our goals, specifically New Year's Resolutions, often isn't enough.

In fact, according to the *US News & World Report*, the failure rate for New Year's resolutions is about 80 percent, and most lose their resolve by mid-February.[28] This news probably does not come as a shock to most of us. How many of us have failed to keep those new year's resolutions? Our intentions are good, but they often don't match up to our actions. Every year, we make new resolutions and fail to keep them. And every year, we give ourselves rational reasons to achieve our goals, and we find ourselves no better off. To understand how to help us become better versions of ourselves, we must first understand what prevents us from achieving our better selves.

Positive behavior change is a complicated hurdle to overcome. After all, we wouldn't have such significant health, wellness, and financial issues if this challenge were easy. Behavior change is a hurdle that products in the health, finance, and education fields face. You're asking users to do something today that may or may not have benefits in the distant future. The payoffs from these actions are often years down the road, and in some instances, not even guaranteed.

In this chapter, we're first going to analyze the psychological headwinds preventing us from meeting our future selves—the forces working against us when we're asked to make decisions that have long-term implications. In the subsequent chapters, we'll look at the behavioral theories you can use to counter the headwinds working against your users. But before we do that, let's go back in time.

Imagine one of your prehistoric ancestors, let's say it is your great grandfather times one hundred—we'll call him

---

28 Marla Tabaka, "Most People Fail to Achieve Their New Year's Resolution. For Success, Choose a Word of the Year Instead."

Aaron. Aaron leads a simple life centered around taking care of his family and his daily hunt for food. Aaron wakes each morning with the sun, sharpens his stone that attaches to his wooden stick, throws on his freshly groomed sheepskin garments, and heads out for the day's hunt. He has one goal—to find food for him and his family.

Aaron is a determined man and always keeps a level head, knowing that some days are destined to be better than others. And some days, Aaron doesn't do so well. He exerts all of his effort hunting, chasing around wild animals, only to come back to his family empty-handed. But Aaron is determined and, on other days, he does better than expected, hunting more game than he and his family need. Without any way to preserve the food, his family has no choice but to have a massive feast.

For many generations, life was much the same for Aaron and all of Aaron's descendants and friends, so much that Aaron's "feel-good-now" behavior became the natural way he operated. Over thousands upon thousands of years, these tendencies did not disappear, and our preference for instant gratification still holds today.[29] We want to feel good right now rather than wait to receive a benefit in the future, even if that future benefit is greater than the benefit we would receive today. This idea is the underpinning of any application where you're asking users to take an action today (e.g., eat healthy, exercise, save money, etc.) that has a long-term, and often uncertain benefit.

It's not that we don't want to live better lives. We all want to be healthier, smarter, and wealthier, but our current selves have a difficult time meeting our future selves. Our future

---

29 Franklin Templeton Investments, Present Bias—Investor Behavior.

self always seems to be fleeting. So what exactly is going on here?

We have a bias toward the present, giving stronger weight to present payoffs than those that will happen in the future. As we think into the future, we view ourselves differently.

Psychology has looked at the way we think about our future selves compared to our current selves.[30] Our perception of ourselves change over time, from first person to third person.[31] Today I think of myself in terms of "I," but I view my future self as "he."

Some research suggests that the way we perceive our future selves is similar to the way that we perceive a stranger.[32] It is an odd concept, but one could argue that because of this, what happens to our future selves is as inconsequential as that thing happening to a random person we've never met. My current self would love to have enough money saved for retirement, but whether my future self has enough money saved is as inconsequential to me as the retirement savings of a random person I pass on the street.

Present Bias ties into another theory, Hyperbolic Discounting, which states that we have time-inconsistent preferences.[33]

Imagine you're sitting in your living room when your good friend arrives home from the grocery store. He is attempting to meal plan for the coming week and mentions that he will have leftover chocolate and oranges at the end

---

30 Sarah Molouki, "Increasing The Pull Of The Future Self."
31 Emily Pronin and Lee Ross, "Temporal differences in trait self-ascription: when the self is seen as an other." 197-209.
32 Emily Pronin, Christopher Y. Olivola, and Kathleen A. Kennedy, "Doing unto future selves as you would do unto others: Psychological distance and decision making." 224-236.
33 David Laibson, "Golden eggs and hyperbolic discounting." 443-478.

of next week. He kindly asks if you'd like an orange or a chocolate bar next week.

The only caveat is that you must decide right now what you'd prefer next week. You select the orange; you want to eat healthily, and the pleasure from eating the chocolate bar doesn't seem worth it considering the extra calories you'll consume.

Now, imagine the same scenario, but instead of asking which item you'll have a week from now, he offers to give you one right now. Do your preferences flip? Is the chocolate bar right now more tempting than the chocolate bar in a week?

It's an interesting thought experiment, and it's one that Read and van Leeuwen found interesting too. When they asked participants to choose fruit or chocolate for the next week, 74 percent chose fruit. However, when they changed the scenario and asked if they would like fruit or chocolate to consume today, 70 percent chose chocolate.[34]

The thought of eating a chocolate bar now gives me instant pleasure, so I ignore the negatives, such as the extra calories. Postponing the outcome of the decision removes the opportunity for instant gratification, thus making it easier to conclude that the extra calories are not worth the fleeting pleasure. This is why it's easier for me to put off eating a chocolate bar a week from now rather than right now. The pleasure I derive from eating the chocolate is discounted.

Hyperbolic Discounting is our tendency to discount options on a hyperbolic curve, whether positive or negative, as they move into the future. As options move even hours or days into the future, our perceived value of those options

---

34 Daniel Read and Barbara Van Leeuwen, "Predicting hunger: The effects of appetite and delay on choice." 189-205.

sharply declines. The further into the future these options exist, the more substantial the discount.

Time is odd, and we don't view it linearly. Even though an hour today is the same length as an hour a week from today, psychologically, it's quite different. We discount pain and pleasure as they move into the future quite heavily, even when the payoff is only hours from the present moment. The idea of exercising for an hour right now is much harder to stomach than having to work out for an hour in a week from today.[35]

We discount both gains and losses. The further out into the future the loss or gain happens, the more heavily we discount it. Enticing people to save for retirement is difficult because we discount the value of our future money. The benefits of retirement savings lives in the distant future so we discount the value of those savings.

I am not stating that the proposed solutions in the following chapters are the silver bullets to solve all the problems we face when it comes to helping us meet our future selves. Nevertheless, through the course of the next section, I'll offer fascinating insights that help move the needle forward and counter the natural forces working against us when it comes to change. Once you understand why we often fail to meet our future selves, you can develop solutions to overcome those challenges.

When building technology that asks an individual to make a decision today that has significant implications for

---

35 Ted O'Donoghue and Matthew Rabin, "Doing it now or later." 103-124.

their future selves, it's important to understand the underlying behavioral mechanisms at play there. Otherwise, you're working against human nature.

To offset Present Bias, we must close the gap between our current selves and our future selves. Is there a way to decrease the psychological distance between our current selves and future selves by compressing space and time? How do we bring our future selves closer to our current selves to shrink this gap? And if we can't close this gap, what techniques can we use to help us move in the right direction?

We'll dig into how methods such as reward systems, gamification models, commitment devices, and goal setting are, at their core, mechanisms to provide a stop-gap in the near-term given that the real reward for taking action is far in the distant future. Armed with an understanding of the underlying currents, we can better build products to swim with the current rather than against it.

CHAPTER 4:

IMAGINING YOUR FUTURE SELF

As I scrolled through my Instagram feed, I began noticing photos of my friends, but they looked oddly different than usual. My friends' faces looked old, ancient.

That's odd, I thought.

After conducting a bit of research, I realized my friends were using FaceApp to alter their images and make it look as if they were an older person. Within weeks, these types of photos littered social media.

FaceApp leverages AI to power a state-of-the-art photo editor and boasts over eighty million active users. The idea is simple, but the effects are powerful—snap or upload a photo of yourself, and after applying any of the twenty-one free filters, the app presents you with a version of your older self.[36]

I decided to download the app and try it myself. I navigated to the AppStore and clicked download, took a selfie,

---

36 "FaceApp."

applied a few filters, and hit submit. After just a few seconds, I was greeted by future Nate, looking about eighty years old. While I anticipated this to be a fun yet straightforward exercise, it had a surprisingly profound effect on me.

As I peered back at myself, my face wrinkly, my hairline receded, I was pleased that I had managed to keep a beautiful shade of grey hair. I looked old, but in a healthy, somewhat charming way, in a way that gave me the sense that I had lived a good life. The image was on par with my expectations, but the feeling gave me pause.

Here I was, staring at a version of myself that seemed to close a gap in time that I had never before confronted. I had never seen, nor imagined what elderly Nate would look like, but now here he was, looking right back at me. With this realization came a sense of responsibility, I couldn't help but wonder what was going through his mind.

"What is he thinking? What is he feeling? What does he know that I should know now? What would my future self tell my current self?" And with this came the realization, "Am I doing everything I can today to help my future self?"

I began to feel an odd sense of accountability toward my future self now that I was face to face with him. Suddenly, I felt concerned for him, a concern that one would feel for a close family member or a good friend. I should be doing everything in my power today to ensure I can fulfill the expectations of the person I was looking at on the screen. And with a simple altered photo, FaceApp had brought my future self to meet my current self.

Neurological studies have found that when thinking about our future self, our brain activity closely resembles our brain activity when thinking about other people.[37]

"Seeing the future self as another person, albeit one who feels close to us now, may allow for more patient, long-term decision-making," Professor Hal Hershfield of UCLA's Anderson School of Management wrote in *Current Opinion in Psychology*. "Seeing the distant future self as an emotional stranger, however, may result in decisions that prioritize today over tomorrow."[38]

We often do not care enough for our future self; we take actions today that negatively impact who we will be down the road. We care in the abstract. After all, why wouldn't we? However, studies have shown that it is difficult for us to connect the dots. Our uncertainties about what will unfold in the future and our tendency to underestimate the pace at which time will progress make it difficult for ourselves today to meet ourselves tomorrow.

Products in the health, finance, and education space are asking users to take actions that will impact their future selves such as eating healthier, exercising more, spending smarter, or learning quicker. Our wiring is such that we care about our current selves, but we don't much show consideration for our future selves.

When building technology, we do not bring our future self closer to our current self, and then we wonder why users

---

37 Hal Ersner-Hershfield, G. Elliott Wimmer, and Brian Knutson, "Saving for the future self: Neural measures of future self-continuity predict temporal discounting." 85.92
38 Hal Ersner-Hershfield, "The self over time." 72-75.

fail to complete the actions we ask of them. Like my experience with FaceApp, bringing one's future self closer to the current self can create a more profound sense of connection to the future version of a person and encourage intentional action toward that future person.

What happens to your future self is as inconsequential as though it is happening to another person. I think of myself today in the first person, but I think about my future self in the third person.[39] Sure, I'd like to save money for retirement for myself today, but whether I do that for my future self could be as inconsequential as if a random stranger has money saved for retirement.

A 2017 study by the Institute for the Future found that the majority of Americans (53 percent) rarely or never think about what life will be like in thirty years.[40] As such, these individuals are unlikely to feel a sense of connectedness with their future selves. Connecting people with their future selves affects their willingness to save for retirement.[41]

Those who perceive more personal stability over time tend to behave in a more future-oriented fashion—one that aligns better with their future self. Research has found that college seniors who were told they would remain more or less the same person after graduation would elect to delay a significant financial reward to a later time compared to students who were told that graduation was a life-altering event.[42]

---

39 Sarah Molouki, "Increasing the Pull of the Future Self."
40 Hal Ersner-Hershfield, et al, "Increasing saving behavior through age-progressed renderings of the future self." S23-S37.
41 Jamie Hopkins, "How to get investors to save more for retirement? Perhaps by saying hello to their future self."
42 Hal Ersner-Hershfield, et al, "Don't stop thinking about tomorrow: Individual differences in future self-continuity account for saving." 280-286.

The feeling FaceApp gave me is one that has been studied by researchers. Professor Hal Hershfield partnered with Daniel Goldstein of Microsoft Research, Jeremy Bailenson from Stanford's Virtual Human Interaction Lab, and several other Stanford researchers to conduct an experiment. They hypothesized that interacting with a vivid visualization of an individual's future self would cause them to increase their retirement savings.

In an attempt to close the gap, the researchers took photos of each participant and altered them to approximate what they would look like at age sixty-five. The final product was an avatar complete with wrinkles, receding hair lines, and grey hairs. Participants were allowed to interact with their "future self" in virtual reality and then asked to allocate some portion of a hypothetical $1,000 reward to their retirement savings.

On average, participants who experienced a virtual version of their future selves were willing to put away roughly double for retirement.[43] Virtual reality augmentation has been applied outside of the research lab.

AARP (American Association of Retired Persons) is the nation's largest nonprofit, nonpartisan organization dedicated to empowering Americans fifty and older to choose how they live as they age.[44] As of 2018, it had more than thirty-eight million members. AARP helps people save for retirement and is familiar of the headwinds working against their members when they are asked to save.

Incorporating this approach, AARP put the research to the test and released an app, quite like FaceApp, where

---

43 Jean Hagan, "Survey Finds Majority of Americans Don't Think about the Future."
44 "About AARP."

retirees used augmented reality to see what they might look like in thirty years.

Our future selves are so often fleeting, the closer we get to them, the further in the distance they are. This chapter highlighted several ways you can start to close the gap to make future selves seem more current. Knowing the underlying psychology, I challenge you to imagine other ways you can help your users meet their future selves.

CHAPTER 5:

DESIRE TO ACHIEVE

On May 16, 2010, with the United States Capitol in the background, I sat with thousands of my classmates on the lawn of the National Mall, flanked by friends and family, all here to celebrate a monumental achievement. We had survived four years of pulling all-nighters, writing papers, and frankly, partying. I was mere moments from becoming a proud graduate of The George Washington University and entering the real world.

Up until that point in my life, letter grades and GPAs measured efforts. The motivation to learn wasn't necessarily driven by the pursuit of knowledge but rather by the desire to see a 4.0 GPA on my report card. Mentors taught us that this was the key to a prosperous career and a happy life.

The pressure to succeed in the academic space spares no one. You're always in competition with your peers, but more importantly, with yourself. A concrete number or a letter grade measures your progress indicating to the world how well or poorly you are progressing in the educational game. For many, they are chasing external rewards such as the desire to be the top of their class, to be crowned valedictorian, achieve a perfect 4.0 GPA, or graduate summa cum laude. These are known as extrinsic motivators, encouraging the completion of an activity in exchange for an external reward. We see these types of rewards extend beyond the classroom in the form of pay raises, promotions, bonuses, extra benefits, prizes, and many others.[45]

When the reward is too far off in the distant future, you need a substitution to fill the void. Rather than asking people to make a trade-off between pain now and a benefit later, give them a benefit now in the form of an external reward. Study hard today, and I'll give you an A.

Julie O'Brien, Director of Behavior Change at WW (formerly Weight Watchers), thinks about it this way, "The way a lot of behavioral scientists think about incentives is reward substitution. The reward is further out into the future, which is usually not salient to people; they're not thinking about it, it's too abstract, too uncertain, and the cost right now is salient and certain."

For others, getting perfect grades isn't the motivator, but rather a yearning deep inside themselves for learning. The pure enjoyment of learning motivates them, deriving satisfaction from completing a challenging math problem, participating in a philosophical debate, or understanding how democracy came to be. While they achieve high marks on exams, the need to see a 4.0 GPA on their report card doesn't drive their need to succeed. An intrinsic motivator is where one genuinely derives a feeling of satisfaction from completing the task itself rather than a reward received for the task. The task provides the person with a sense of enjoyment, purpose, growth, curiosity, passion, self-expression, and fun.

---

45 Laura Hamill and Toni Best, "Watch Webinar on Demand: The Power of Intrinsic Motivation."

As evident by my grades throughout school, intrinsic motivators drove me more so than extrinsic ones. The classes I performed the best in were the classes I genuinely enjoyed. While grades motivated me to do well, they did so only to a point. The potential for high marks wouldn't push me to score an A in a class I genuinely did not find interesting.

For most of us, our educational experience is a blend of both types of motivators. We fall somewhere on the spectrum of being extrinsically motivated by rewards and intrinsically motivated by the enjoyment we receive from learning itself.

While intrinsic and extrinsic motivators incentivize us differently, the desire to achieve is wired into our DNA.[46] We set out to meet specific benchmarks when there is a tangible reward such as a pay bonus or social recognition, but we will also work hard if we genuinely enjoy the activity itself.

Rewards are complicated, though, both extrinsic and intrinsic. When and how to use reward frameworks varies depending on what you are incentivizing, as we will see in this chapter.

Rewards drive and reinforce action—an idea that Burrhus Frederic (B.F.) Skinner pioneered. Skinner believed free will is an illusion; we act in accordance with the consequences our actions produce. If we take action and we receive a reward, there is a high chance we will take that action again. If we take action and the consequences are bad, there is a high

---

[46] Edward L. Deci, Richard Koestner, and Richard M. Ryan, "A meta-analytic review of experiments examining the effects of extrinsic rewards on intrinsic motivation." 627-668.

chance we won't repeat the action. He believed that through this framework, humans could be conditioned to take a desired action.[47]

Operant conditioning is a learning process in which we learn new behaviors via their association with consequences. Reinforce a behavior with a reward, and we associate the reward with the behavior. We learn that to receive the reward again, you must do the same behavior. We do well in a class and receive an A, so we learn to repeat the behaviors that earned us an A. The next time we take a class, we repeat the behavior to obtain the reward.[48]

Skinner, along with C.B. Ferster, researched the various ways to reinforce behaviors over a given period, the "Schedule of Reinforcements." He believed you can condition animals and people to perform or not perform specific tasks by altering the associated reward or punishment.[49]

The most common deployment of Skinner's work is in the field of habit building. Reinforce an action by linking it to a reward, and one learns over time: If I do x, I receive y. I enjoy y, so if I do x again, I'll receive more of y.

This reward cycle is a fundamental building block of a habit and is broken into multiple steps. The trigger signals you to do the action. You wake up in the morning with a bad taste in your mouth. The action is what you do following the trigger. In this instance, you pick up the mouthwash. The

---

[47] Kendra Cherry, "B.F. Skinner Biography: One Leader of Behaviorism."
[48] Saul McLeod, "Skinner—Operant Conditioning."
[49] Kendra Cherry, "B.F. Skinner Biography: One Leader of Behaviorism."

investment is either time, money, effort, or social capital that you invest in the action. Here, you rinse your mouth with minty mouth wash. Then, you receive a reward—the fresh-breath feeling. This reward reinforces the action you took and begins to build the habit loop.

In the absence of the reward, the fresh-breath feeling, you stop rinsing your mouth with mouthwash. The fresh-breath feeling does not contribute to cleaning your mouth. It's purely there as a reward to reinforce the action. You rinse your mouth because you want that fresh-breath feeling.

Nir Eyal's book, *Hooked: How to Build Habit-Forming Products*, examines the habit loop in the context of product design. If this is an area of specific interest to you, I recommend grabbing a copy of Nir's book; it digs into great detail about this framework in product design.[50]

Nir notes that the reward should be variable, and there should be an investment component where the user puts something into the product such as time, data, effort, social capital, or money. Effort increases the chance that the user will repeat this action in the future.[51] You receive a push notification on your phone (trigger) that asks you to categorize a recent banking expense. You then click on the link (action) to classify the banking expense (investment). You then receive a virtual badge (reward) for completing the action. Nir believes building habit loops into products is a tried-and-tested technique to get users to come back and use your app over and over again.

Let's explore how and when to deploy rewards, the difference between how extrinsic and intrinsic motivators are

---

50   Nir Eyal, *Hooked: How to Build Habit-Forming Products*.
51   Ibid.

used, and why understanding how and when to use various reward paradigms is critical to ensure you're encouraging the right behavior.

When Julie O'Brien was a team member at Opower, a company that partners with utilities to engage their customers through energy reports, Julie noted a trend in the market at the time for every service provider to have some type of loyalty program.

Her job was to figure out how to create a rewards program that not only looked great but was also effective. It wasn't as simple as just building a rewards program and then rewarding customers for the actions you want them to take. Therefore, before making the program, Julie and her team dug into the academic research and conducted extensive testing to set Opower up for success.

Her team ran a study to identify which of the twenty-five behaviors to reward. They theorized that not every behavior *should* be incentivized because not every behavior *can* be incentivized. They asked people to rate all the actions that Opower was considering incentivizing and asked them how easy it was to perform that action. For example, they asked how easy it was for them to buy a new refrigerator, change their lightbulbs, do an energy audit, etc., and then asked them how intrinsically motivated they were to do each action.

Julie added, "Ultimately, what we wanted to know was what predicts when incentives work and when they backfire."

Julie notes that the story was beautiful, clean, and replicated the academic literature she had researched. External rewards motivated customers in certain instances. The action had to be easy, such as changing a lightbulb, and the person shouldn't already have an intrinsic motivation to do the task. A hard task motivated by intrinsic motivation—such as a customer saving energy because they care about the environment—external rewards are ineffective.

WW, previously known as Weight Watchers, shifted its focus from weight to wellness with the re-branding as WW and the tagline, "Wellness that Works."[52] The program leverages both extrinsic and intrinsic motivators to nudge their members to build long-term healthy habits.

WW started in the early 1960s by Jean Nidetch when Jean decided to invite a group of friends to her New York City home to discuss the best ways to lose weight. What started as a small group of friends would evolve into a core part of the past and current WW programs.

As a member, WW grants you access to a myriad of offline and online tools. One core component of the experience is WellnessWins, which rewards members for small steps they take toward their goals. WW states that this program is "a first-of-its-kind rewards program that celebrates your healthy habits."

Upon login, a Wins Dashboard greets me. This dashboard has ways for me to earn "wins" by tracking easy-to-do and easy-to-track tasks such as what I had for lunch or dinner. I can earn points for physical activities from running and resistance training to "activity in disguise," such as gardening or cleaning the house.[53] Just like credit card points, my wins are traded in to redeem products and services such

---

52 Chrissy Carroll, "What Is Weight Watchers?"
53 "Everything you need to know about FitPoints."

as fitness class passes, travel shoe bags, go-anywhere wine bottles, among many other prizes. I notice how WW rewards activities rather than pounds lost, a key component of building an effective rewards system. The program is keen on rewarding inputs rather than outputs.

Rewards and incentives don't necessarily have to be financial. "When we say incentives, that could mean congratulating somebody or smiling at them and telling them we approve of their behavior," said Julie. Giving users virtual rewards of no monetary value can inspire action.

In an article in *Computers in Human Behavior* by Juho Hamari entitled, "Do Badges Increase User Activity? A Field Experiment on the Effects of Gamification," Hamari worked with the people behind www.sharetribe.com to test how implementing badges would impact user engagement. The website helps users find others to whom they can rent, sell, or share things like products, services, or physical spaces to. Would adding virtual achievements in the form of badges displayed on user profiles increase engagement?

Hamari and his team conducted a field study of almost three thousand actual website visitors in which half of the users received badges for certain tasks while the other half did not. When analyzing results between the two groups, Hamari found that badges increased the likelihood that any given user would use the website. Results showed that users in the gamified condition were significantly more likely to "post-trade proposals, carry out transactions, comment on proposals, and generally use the service more actively."[54]

---

54 Juho Hamari, "Do badges increase user activity? A field experiment on the effects of gamification." 469-478.

Rewards are an effective way to drive behavior, but we adjust and become accustomed to rewards over time. Once we obtain a reward, we reach for the next best thing. The first time we receive a $1,000 bonus at work, it feels amazing. We're ecstatic, jumping up and down and imagining where we will spend our bonus. The second time, we may still feel great, but it fails to provide the same high as the first time. By the tenth time, the reward brings us little joy. We're accustomed to receiving the reward and the excitement wore off.

According to Robert Sapolsky's *Behave: The Biology of Humans at Our Best and Worst*, humans are neurologically wired to be dissatisfied, to continually strive, and to want more.[55]

Dopamine is the high you get from experiencing something new and exciting. Yes, dopamine makes you feel good, but there is a drawback. You can't get enough. The more you get, the more you want. The reward you got yesterday becomes your new baseline.

The nervous system produces dopamine during the experience of reward, but even more interesting is that the production of dopamine also happens in anticipation of a reward. As Robert Sapolsky states, "Once reward contingencies are learned, dopamine is less about reward than about its anticipation." Anticipating the reward can be more fulfilling than actually receiving the reward.[56]

If this is true, how can we increase anticipation?

---

55   Robert M. Sapolsky, *Behave: The Biology of Humans at Our Best and Worst*.
56   Nate Andorsky, "Why We're Never Satisfied—It's All in the Wiring."

Taking a page out of the gamble machine in Las Vegas, we can give rewards based on an unpredictable schedule. The anticipation of if and when we'll receive a reward can have a greater effect on driving behavior than the reward itself.

Skinner invented the operant conditioning chamber, also known as the Skinner Box, to study this idea. Using these tools, Skinner and C.B. Ferster produced their most influential experimental work, which appeared in their book, *Schedules of Reinforcement*.[57, 58]

Imagine a box large enough to hold a small animal such as a mouse. This box contains a food dispenser, an electrified grid, a speaker, lights, and a response lever. It allows experimenters to study behavior by training the animal to perform certain actions. The mouse presses the lever in response to a sight or sound stimuli, and after the mouse performs the behavior, the box rereleases food rewards through the dispenser.

Skinner found the Variable Schedule of Reinforcements to be extremely effective. In this system, he varied how often the subject received a reward after the subject completed the target behavior. He would sometimes reward an animal after it took action, and sometimes he wouldn't. Skinner discovered that the anticipation of the reward, not the reward itself, motivates the subject. Pigeons can become compulsive gamblers just as humans can by reinforcing them in the right way.[59]

---

57 Kendra Cherry, "B.F. Skinner Biography: One Leader of Behaviorism."
58 Charles B. Ferster and Burrhus Frederic Skinner, Schedules of Reinforcement. 1957.
59 Burrhus Frederic Skinner, "Superstition in the pigeon." 168.

You may notice this technique in various social networks that leverage notifications. Website such as Facebook will hold back likes and drip them out according to an Intermediate Variable Reinforcement (IVR) schedule. What draws the user in is not necessarily the like itself but the anticipation of when the next like will come. The closer we get to receiving a reward and missing it, the more likely we are to engage in said behavior again.

Any website that has a feed may leverage this approach. To keep us engaged as we scroll, rather than showing us all good, relevant updates, these sites may show several uninteresting things with one great thing. We continue to scroll hoping to stumble upon another juicy update in a sea of mediocre content. The anticipation of whether or not we'll stumble across something exciting keeps us hooked. If you see success with an incentive program, it could be worth exploring this type of model to strengthen it.

Counter to extrinsic motivators, intrinsic motivators are not tangible and therefore difficult to measure and implement. The reward is a feeling we receive after completing an activity rather than a badge on a screen or a gift card to Chipotle. Although these rewards come from within us, they are not any less motivating. Intrinsic motivators are self-reinforcing and they have long-lasting effects.

Daniel Pink, a *New York Times* bestselling author, shatters the way we think about human motivation. Common belief has been that the best way to motivate people is by the carrot and the stick approach. Do the right thing, get rewarded, do the wrong thing, get punished, but that is not always necessarily true.[60]

Daniel argues that for straightforward tasks, ones which are well-defined and repetitive, a carrot and a stick approach does work—for example, motivating someone to produce a certain number of widgets in an hour. Daniel's argument mirrors Julie Obrien's findings in her work with Opower.

However, intrinsic motivation drives creative tasks that are open to interpretation. He draws on four decades of scientific research on human motivation, identifies the mismatch between what science knows and what business does, and examines the three elements he believes make up true motivation: autonomy, mastery, and purpose.

He highlights this with a story about Microsoft's failed encyclopedia product called *Encarta*.[61]

"In the mid-1990s, Microsoft started an encyclopedia called *Encarta*. They had deployed all the right incentives, and they paid professionals to write and edit thousands of articles. Well-compensated managers oversaw the whole thing to make sure it came in on budget and on time. A few years later, another encyclopedia got started with a different model: do it for fun. No one gets paid a cent or a euro or a yen. Do it because you like to do it." said Daniel.

"Just ten years ago, if you had gone to an economist anywhere, 'Hey, I've got these two different models for creating an encyclopedia. If they went head to head, who would win?' Ten years ago, you could not have found a single sober economist anywhere on planet Earth who would have predicted the Wikipedia model," Daniel adds.

---

60 Daniel H. Pink, Drive: The Surprising Truth about What Motivates Us (Penguin, 2011).
61 Daniel H. Pink, "The puzzle of motivation."

Today, *Encarta* does not exist while Wikipedia develops at a rate of over 1.8 edits per second, performed by editors from all over the world. The English Wikipedia includes 6,019,467 articles with an average of 572 new articles per day.[62]

"This is the titanic battle between these two approaches. This is the Ali-Frazier of motivation, right? This is the Thrilla in Manila. Intrinsic motivators versus extrinsic motivators. Autonomy, mastery, and purpose versus carrot and sticks, and who wins? Intrinsic motivation, autonomy, mastery, and purpose, in a knockout," says Daniel.

As evidenced throughout this chapter, it can be difficult to determine when and how to integrate a rewards system. After all, if they both seem to work, wouldn't incorporating both intrinsic and extrinsic rewards be powerful?

A paper in the *Journal of Personality and Social Psychology* looked at this. Researchers conducted a field experiment with three- to five-year-old nursery school children to test the "over-justification" hypothesis—intrinsic interest decreases when introducing an extrinsic reward.[63] Researchers selected fifty-one students who already showed an intrinsic interest in an activity and exposed them to one of three conditions.

Researchers asked the students to draw a picture. In the first condition, no reward was given to the students for drawing pictures. In the second condition, researchers rewarded

---

62 Wikipedia.
63 Mark R. Lepper, David Greene, and Richard E. Nisbett, "Undermining children's intrinsic interest with extrinsic reward: A test of the 'over-justification' hypothesis." 129-137.

students in the form of a gold star only after completing their drawing. However, the students did not know the potential reward before engaging in the activity.

In the third condition, researchers told students they would receive a gold star upon completion of their drawing. These students were aware of the potential reward before starting the activity. In this condition, students showed less subsequent intrinsic interest in the drawing activity. There seemed to be a crowding-out effect. By informing students of their external reward before starting their activity, intrinsic motivation decreased.

———

While it's clear how to trigger extrinsically motivated behaviors, intrinsically motivated behaviors are difficult to trigger. After all, the motivation comes from within us, not from an external reward.

One idea is using external rewards as a stopgap to build intrinsic motivation, Julie adds, "One idea is to taper off incentives over time."

As a child, you may have never wanted to play the piano, so your parents had to offer you a reward for practicing. Over time, you developed a passion for music and found yourself continuing to play in the absence of a tangible reward. This had now become part of your identity, your sense of self. Without the external motivator, you may have never discovered the passion you had for music in the first place.

Julie adds, "People are motivated to do things that reflect their sense of self, and once it becomes part of your sense of self, it becomes more intrinsic."

Another idea to trigger intrinsic motivation comes from a study of high school students.

Researchers randomly selected 1,982 high school students and asked them to give motivational advice to younger students. We'll call them "advice-givers." The "advice-givers" never met the students face to face. Rather, they completed fourteen open-ended and multiple-choice questions in which they advised younger students on optimal study locations and study strategies. The advice-givers wrote a motivational letter to an anonymous younger student who wanted to do better in school.

Interestingly, the advice-givers, not the younger students, earned higher report card grades in both math and a self-selected target class over an academic quarter. The research suggests that putting individuals in a position to *give* advice could enhance their intrinsic motivation to do well themselves. Giving advice, not receiving it, motivated achievement.

The researchers are not sure of the exact mechanisms that accounted for the effect, but based on past research, they have a few ideas. The technique mitigates the cognitive dissonance for the advice-givers; if they're giving advice, they want to align themselves with the beliefs they are instilling in the younger students. If we're going to make a recommendation to someone else, we're inclined to follow what we're telling others. Finally, giving advice boosted the advice-givers' confidence. After all, if the advice-givers were the "experts" helping others succeed, they must know what they are doing.[64]

---

64 Lauren Eskreis-Winkler, et al, "A large-scale field experiment shows giving advice improves academic outcomes for the advisor." 14808-14810.

In terms of product design, this same concept can be used to spark intrinsic motivation by asking users to advise another user before embarking on a task. For example, a prompt that reads, "Before beginning this educational lesson, what tips would you give other users to ensure they complete their lesson?"

In the context of learning specifically, rewards and their implementation are still a highly debated topic, as noted in this Student Success guide, "Experts are split on which kind of motivation, extrinsic or intrinsic, has a greater impact on a learning environment."[65]

Incentives are critical, and the manner of deployment is just as important. There is still much research and testing to be done when it comes to rewards, but there are already practical approaches even in its infancy.

It is important to first consider the desired action before you integrate the reward. If the desired action is a task that involves mastery and purpose, it would make sense to explore intrinsic motivators. However, if it is a specific, relatively easy task with a concrete outcome, easy to do, and with an endpoint, extrinsic motivators would be a good place to start.

―――

The approach we have taken at Creative Science is to continually test and iterate various approaches. A good rule of thumb is to leverage external rewards to promote interest in an activity that is easy but may not initially interest a user. Then, if possible, trigger intrinsic motivations to reinforce the action over the long term.

---

65   "Student Success Guide: Extrinsic vs. Intrinsic Motivation."

External or internal rewards, when and how to use which—it's complicated. Both types of rewards work differently in different contexts. In some instances, these two approaches can work well together, and in other cases, they can have adverse effects on one another. The vital lesson to remember is to dig into the academic literature, test, test, and test, and help your users stay motivated.

CHAPTER 6:

BRIDGING THE GAP BETWEEN INTENTION AND ACTION

It's 10 a.m. on Saturday, September 14. It's a beautiful morning, and I am at my kitchen table, music playing in the background, with a crisp fall breeze blowing through the windows. I am enjoying a cold brew from my local coffee shop and typing away on my computer, striving to hit a deadline that is quickly approaching. By Sunday, September 15, 2019, I had promised my editor I would write at least fifteen thousand words.

As of last night, I had written about ten thousand words, leaving me with five thousand words to hit my goal. With a little under twenty-four hours to go, I am confident I'll hit my deadline. The goal is specific (fifteen thousand words) and attainable. I am only five thousand words away.

My future self wants to be an author, but my current self is fighting against it for a myriad of reasons. Having a completed manuscript is so vast and far off in the distant future that it doesn't seem attainable or concrete. It lives in the abstract.

Every time I sit down to begin writing, I remember how far I am from the finish line. Writing a few pages feels futile. Writing a book is a large and seemingly unattainable task (trust me), but as I woke up this morning, I asked myself if I could write another five thousand words before the day is over.

My editor asks me to commit to smaller, attainable, concrete goals that are not far in the distant future and reminds me not to let perfection become the enemy of progress.

I have a specific benchmark to hit, but not only that, it is attainable and concrete. I can concretely see my future self writing five thousand words by the end of Sunday. So, here I am on word 10,698, with only a little more than four thousand to go.

Our intentions are good—eat healthier, save money, exercise more—but our actions don't line up with our intentions. We intend to do positive things in the future, but when that future moment arises, we fail to follow through. We are not unaware of our difficulty achieving better versions of our future selves and we have created commitment devices to increase the likelihood that we will follow through on our intentions.

Commitment devices help us follow through on our intentions. At their core, these devices are an agreement made today to complete a task in the future. According to journalist Stephen J. Dubner and economist Steven Levitt, commitment devices are "a way to lock yourself into following a plan of action that you might not want to do, but you know is good for you."[66]

---

66 Stephen J. Dubner and Steven D. Levitt, "The Stomach-Surgery Conundrum."

One of the simplest of observations as to why goal setting and commitment devices work is that conscious human behavior is purposeful- it is regulated by our goals.[67] Research has shown that using commitment devices increases our likelihood to follow through on intention. It closes what is known as the intention-action gap, the difference between what we *say* we will do compared what we *actually* do.[68]

Commitment devices have two major features. First, they are voluntary. If participation is required, it isn't a commitment device. The participant needs to be given the choice of whether to participate or not. Second, there is a reward for achieving the desired outcome and/or a punishment for failing to achieve the goal.[69]

These devices fall on a spectrum between soft and hard. A soft commitment takes the form of a goal that has no tangible consequence for missing the goal or no direct reward for achieving the goal. Committing to a friend to work out at least five times a week doesn't carry a reward or punishment for not meeting your commitment, but you feel guilty for letting a friend down.

Hard commitment devices have a tangible consequence or reward tied to them. For example, you commit to donating $10 to charity for every day you don't exercise for at least twenty minutes. This type of approach is also known as a deposit contract or commitment contract; it involves people

---

67 Edwin A. Locke and Gary P. Latham, *A Theory of Goal Setting & Task Performance.*
68 Timothy A. Pychyl, "Closing the Intention-Action Gap."
69 Todd Rogers, Katherine L. Milkman, and Kevin G. Volpp, "Commitment devices: using initiatives to change behavior." 2065-2066.

voluntarily depositing money into accounts that they can only access if they hit their goal.[70]

Eighty-one percent of large employers provide incentives for healthy behavior change, according to one survey.[71] If an employee does x, they will receive y, but could a commitment device prove to be more effective than rewards to drive healthy behaviors?

Quitting smoking is hard. Smokers know the reasons they should give up smoking, but reasons themselves are not enough. Every year, smoking kills more than 480,000 Americans and contributes to more than $170 billion in direct medical care for adults.[72] According to the CDC, tobacco remains the single largest preventable cause of death and disease in the United States.

In a study, "Put Your Money Where Your Butt Is: A Commitment Savings Account for Smoking Cessation," researchers Xavier Giné, Dean Karlan, and Jonathan Zinman designed and tested a voluntary commitment device to help smokers quit.[73]

A common form of a commitment device involves a person voluntarily giving up something of value that they can only regain access to by following through on their commitment.[74] Researchers designed and tested a voluntary commitment

---

70 Ibid.
71 Randel K. Johnson, "Winning With Wellness."
72 "Tips From Former Smokers: All Groups (General Public)."
73 Xavier Giné, Dean Karlan, and Jonathan Zinman, "Put your money where your butt is: a commitment contract for smoking cessation." 213-235.
74 Todd Rogers, Katherine L. Milkman, and Kevin G. Volpp, "Commitment devices: using initiatives to change behavior." 2065-2066.

product (CARES) to aid smokers in quitting. The researchers gave smokers the opportunity to sign a commitment contract where participants would deposit money into CARES and would receive their savings back if they passed a cotinine (the primary metabolite of nicotine) test six months later.

This approach taps into loss aversion, which is our tendency to prefer avoiding losses to acquiring equivalent gains. Psychologically, the pain of losing $20 is equal to gaining $10. With this in mind, it's more effective to structure a commitment contract where the reward money is theirs to lose rather than gain.

If participants passed the test, they got their money back. If they failed, the money would be donated to charity. A second group received "cue cards," which depicted visually aversive pictures of the harmful effects of smoking.

When offered the commitment contract, 11 percent of smokers signed up and committed an average of 550 pesos ($11 USD) over the six months, which is roughly equal to the out-of-pocket expense for cigarettes. While there was no evidence that cue cards had an impact on helping smokers quit, the smokers who signed the contract saw success; they were 3.3 to 5.8 percentage points more likely to pass the six-month urine test compared to the control group. Commitment contracts don't always have to come in the form of money, though. These commitments can be to another person or a group of people.

Even when knowing what we want to achieve, we often don't behave in a way that is conducive to achieving it. We face two main problems in goal setting. First, we often don't set deadlines optimally, and second, we set goals that focus on outputs rather than the necessary inputs.[75]

---

75   Dan Ariely and Klaus Wertenbroch, "Procrastination, deadlines, and performance: Self-control by precommitment." 219-224.

Ever stumble across a crowdfunding campaign that is 90 percent complete and feel the urge to give? You're motivated to give because you can see your donation helping push the campaign over the finish line. Goals should not be so big or far in the distant future that they feel unattainable. Goal gradient theory states that the closer we are to a goal, the more motivated we are to achieve it; this is why it is critical to create goals that feel achievable.[76] One key to achieving your goals is to set evenly spaced, intermittent deadlines along the path to achieve your goals.

As humans, we are wired for growth and intermediary deadlines provide a sense of progress, movement, and accomplishment during the journey toward our future selves. Part of what fuels our willingness to keep pursuing a goal is the feedback we get from achieving the action. We do an action, and we see a reward. If we do an action (put in effort toward learning a language), but we don't see the reward right away (becoming smarter), we begin to wonder why we're doing the action. What's the point?

This is a direct application of Ariely & Wertenbroch's (2002) findings of the importance of intermittent goal-setting to mitigate present bias. They found that people were willing to set self-imposed deadlines to mitigate procrastination but were poor at setting those goals in such a way for optimal performance.[77]

---

[76] Matt Trower, Catherine J. Berman, and Jamie Foehl, "B.E. For Dogs: Goal Gradient."

[77] Dan Ariely and Klaus Wertenbroch, "Procrastination, deadlines, and performance: Self-control by precommitment." 219-224.

Peer Insight is an innovation firm located in Washington, DC, comprised of a team of brilliant problem solvers. They partner with change-makers to create "net-new" growth from products and services beyond a company's existing portfolio.

One of those change-makers is Lauri Kien Kotcher, who, in the mid-2000s, was the SVP of Marketing for Pfizer Consumer Health. Lauri had a weak product in her portfolio: Nicorette. The patch-or-gum nicotine replacement therapy was experiencing weak sales and customer outcomes. She was at a crossroads: kill the product, or… turn it into part of a successful smoking cessation service?

She shared this idea with Peer Insight, and they code-named the project "Pavlov." The Peer Insight team helped Pfizer conduct a year-long market experiment to hypothesize, test, and iterate on a "quit service" that would use Nicorette. A crucial part of the process was to collect SAY and DO data to understand the root of the problem (the WHY).

Smoking cessation research had shown that the average smoker made five or more separate attempts to quit the habit. Despite this pattern of failure, the Pavlov team discovered that much younger (age twenty-five to thirty-five) smokers expressed a conviction that they weren't addicted to nicotine. Instead, their smoking habit was "a lifestyle choice." And they said that someday soon, they would make a different choice.

The DO data suggested something fairly different. Smokers would plan for their quit attempt months in advance, trying to find the time to amass the energy as if for a big fight. The time window after the Super Bowl and before finals was popular with smokers in their twenties. Some would keep their attempt to quit a secret, not talking to any of their friends about their plans. Others would pull all the stops, enrolling friends and coworkers, starting an exercise program, etc. These DO behaviors betrayed a palpable fear of failure.

With each smoking quit failure, the gap between quit attempts grew. One key challenge was how to address the fear of failure, part of what was driving the smoker's reluctance to make another quit attempt. Tim and his team knew that the SAY and DO data were not giving them the full picture, so they began decoding the WHY data.

They hypothesized that the lack of near-term relevance was also an issue. While these smokers knew the long-term hazards of smoking, the negative impacts of smoking weren't being felt by them today; they were far off in the distant future. Doctors, family members, and others frequently chastised smokers, warning them of the harmful effects of smoking. Showing an image of what their lungs would look like in thirty years didn't have much of an impact. Images of medical professionals in lab coats evoked eye rolls.

How could they address this paradox of what smokers SAY (I'm not addicted…those risks are a long way off) and what smokers DO (saving up energy for a BIG fight)? What seemed to lurk just offstage was a deep fear they would fail yet again. What if, instead of them believing, *"Leave me alone. I can do this,"* what they were feeling was, *"OMG, I'm afraid I can't do this, and no one can help me?"* Were these people in their twenties and early thirties imagining a life sentence of smoking?

Based on the Lurking Fear hypothesis, the team reframed the service as a gym membership instead of a medical intervention. What if they provided the smoker with a commitment device, a coach and teammates who would encourage them instead of scolding them? Perhaps they didn't need a different form of reprimand but an *ally*. Someone who would be by their side to encourage them along the path and help mitigate their fear of failure, which came in the form of a Quit Coach. As part of this program, smokers have access to a live one-on-one coach helping guide them through their journey.

In effect, this approach relies on a soft commitment device: the coach and teammates. By asking smokers to commit to another person, the likelihood of failure is much lower. This program combines a text-message phone-based coach and a small cohort of smoker-selected "quit buddies." No longer are smokers only committing to themselves to quit. They are now committing to another person to follow through on their intentions. They tested this approach with thirty-five volunteers, and the outcomes were five times more successful than the Nicorette-only baseline.

The project evolved into the solution that they took to market, branded as ActiveStop. ActiveStop provides a personalized quit coach and an online portal that gives smokers access to resources and customizable quit plans. Most importantly, though, was the ingenious incorporation of a soft commitment device—the one-on-one coach to help them on their journey. The smoker was voluntarily committing to someone they could trust, which increased the likelihood that the smoker would follow through on his or her intention.

Pavlov connected to the underlying WHY and provided a win for the smoker wanting to quit as well as a win for Lori Kien Kotcher and the Pfizer team to make their Nicorette product relevant again. It became Pfizer's first revenue-generating service, and this treatment option is still alive and well today.

Strava is a social fitness network tracking cyclists and runners' activity. Founded in 2009, Mark Gianey and Michael Horvath were looking for a way to help people reach their fitness goals. I decide to take the software for a spin.

Upon logging in, I notice a section that reads, "My Goals—Athletes who set goals spend twice as much time training. Challenge yourself by setting progress, segment, and power goals." This statement is consistent with the academic literature. People who set goals make more progress.

I enter my current location, and I browse through the various routes. Running and biking routes have been populated by other users. With my fitness level in mind, I scroll through the different routes and select the one that suits me best.

As I navigate through the experience, Strava prompts me to set a personal workout goal, so I select a biking route. Strava asks how long it will take me to complete the route. I enter two hours and thirty minutes. Then, it prompts me to input the date by which I'll achieve this goal, defaulting to one month from today if I don't select an option.

Strava prompts me to select a specific goal that is attainable and achievable in the near-term future rather than a general "work at as much as you can" goal. This is a specific and time-limited goal as opposed to a "do your best" goal. Hard but attainable goals drive a higher level of performance than vague goals such as "do your best."[78]

Strava does an excellent job of guiding me to create objectives that encourage me to stay on track while simultaneously

---

78 Edwin A. Locke and Gary P. Latham, *A Theory of Goal Setting & Task Performance.*

allowing me the ability to customize my plan. By letting me set my own goals, it provides me with a sense of ownership over those goals. Research has shown that when individuals set their own goals, they are more likely to accomplish them. Part of this is due to the endowment effect where we place a high value on something we own versus something we don't.

After selecting my goal, complete with a deadline and length, I navigate back to my overview page. I am greeted by the countdown timer which has already started, 29 days, 59 minutes, and 59 seconds. The clock is ticking, so I better get started.

Commitment devices, whether soft or hard, can be extremely powerful. These devices can on take various shapes and sizes and can be integrated into product design in numerous ways. I challenge you to think of groundbreaking ways to incorporate these devices into your product design to help users follow through on their intentions.

CHAPTER 7:

DON'T BREAK THE CHAIN

"Here is a young comedian and he's been working on the road with Andy Williams. Would you welcome Jerry Seinfeld," announced Johnny Carson.[79]

As the white curtain opens, a young Jerry Seinfeld, dressed in a cream-colored suit with a blue tie and a head full of hair, walks onto the stage, arms wide open as if he were welcoming the crowd. The welcome music plays to a welcoming crowd. Moments later, the music fades, and Jerry starts his act.

"Thank you. Thank you very much! I am just happy to be here; I am just happy to be anywhere!" the crowd laughs.

This was the beginning of what would become a long and prosperous career for Jerry Seinfeld; it was his first appearance on Johnny Carson's *Tonight Show*. Alongside Larry David, Jerry would go on to develop the sitcom *Seinfeld,* which would run for nine seasons. By the time the final episode aired in 1998, it was the highest-rated show in the US.

---

79 Johnny Carson, "Jerry Seinfeld's First Appearance on Johnny Carson's Tonight Show."

Born in Brooklyn, New York to Kalman and Betty Seinfeld, Jerry had an early start as a comedian. By age eight, Jerry was putting himself through rigorous comic training, watching television day and night to study the techniques of famous comedians. In a field littered with failed comics who never even had the chance to perform on TV in front of a live studio audience, Jerry managed to make it.[80]

Becoming a great stand-up comedian takes more than talent. It takes a daily dedication to a craft few of us have. As a comedian, coming up with material, let alone funny material, is an arduous and daunting task. Performing a sixty-minute stand-up routine in front of thousands of people can feel so unattainable that one could see how easy it could be to give up.

Jerry had an interesting technique to ensure consistent progress toward his life goals. He used a simple but powerful trick that taps into the way humans are wired. Throughout his career, as he worked to perfect his craft, he committed to writing one joke per day. Every day, one joke. Not an entire routine, not an entire monologue, but simply one joke, every single day.

A large calendar hung on Jerry's apartment wall, and for each day he would write a joke, he would place a large X. The more X's he accumulated, the harder it became for him to break the streak. It served as a visual cue of the hard work he had put in, how far he had come, and a reminder that breaking his streak wouldn't just mean missing a day of joke writing, it would mean losing the streak that he had worked so hard to build. The chain provided Jerry with a sense of progress toward a much larger goal that seemed so far off it could feel as if he wasn't progressing toward that goal at all.[81] But it did

---

80 "Jerry Seinfeld Biography."
81 "Don't Break the Chain—Jerry Seinfeld's Method for Creative Success."

something else. Whether he realized it or not, it tapped into the core of human behavior using a technique that has also been leveraged by one of the most successful online learning platforms.

Over six million Americans are pursuing online education, and that number has risen every year for the past few years. A quarter of all college students are taking online classes.[82] But online education is difficult, and the retention rates are poor. While completion rates have improved over the years for online courses, one thing is for sure—learning online is difficult. Only 5 percent to 15 percent of people who start a free online course end up completing it.[83]

Duolingo touts itself as the best way to learn a language. It is fun and addictive. You can earn points for correct answers and race against the clock to complete a lesson. Their bite-sized teachings are effective, and Duolingo has proof it works. Launched in 2012, Duolingo is now the most popular way to learn languages in the world. With three hundred million users around the globe, Duolingo currently teaches twenty-three distinct languages.[84] More people in the US are learning languages on Duolingo than in the whole public school system.[85] The entire experience is behaviorally informed, and one technique has proven to be effective—their use of streaks.

---

[82] "The who, what, when and why behind online education."
[83] Amy Ahearn, "Moving From 5% to 85% Completion Rates for Online Courses."
[84] Will Smale, "The man teaching 300 million people a new language."
[85] Michaela Kron, "The United States of Languages: An analysis of Duolingo usage state-by-state."

Luis von Ahn, CEO and cofounder of Duolingo, provides insight into his mission, "A lot of people view education as something that brings inequality to different social classes, but I always saw it as the opposite, something that brings equality."[86]

The creators of Duolingo know learning a language is hard, and providing users with rational reasons to learn would be an uphill battle. They have leveraged an understanding of human behavior to increase the likelihood that users would find success on their platform. Like other educational, financial, and health-focused apps, a major behavioral hurdle that prevents lasting change is present bias. In this case, accomplishing the feat of learning a new language is vague, uncertain, and distant. Therefore, the primary focus of Duolingo is to make the long-term benefits of learning a new language more immediately salient.

In Luis' eyes, learning is more than acquiring knowledge. Education unlocks economic opportunity. "If you learn English in a non-English-speaking country, your job prospects increase by a lot. You can make between 25 percent and 100 percent higher salary by just knowing English."[87]

Two behavioral science practitioners, Rachika Komal and Soumya Behuguna, agree with Luis, "Good education is a fundamental human right, but it's still a distant dream in many parts of the world. Education for all, then, is a big goal for the decade. The outlook for democratizing education is positive if we turn to new solutions—online learning."[88]

---

86 Duolingo, "The story behind Duolingo's mission – Luis von Ahn, CEO."
87 Duolingo, "The story behind Duolingo's mission – Luis von Ahn, CEO."
88 Evan Nesterak, "Imagining the Next Decade of Behavioral Science."

I download Duolingo to see what all the rave is about. After downloading, the app prompts me to begin my journey. I select my preferred language (Hebrew), and shortly after, Duolingo's mascot, an owl, can be seen dancing on the screen for a few seconds with text that reads, *"Loading..."*

After asking me to input why I am learning a language (career, school, brain training, etc.), the app asks me to commit to a goal. I select my goal, and I am off to my first lesson. After completing my first daily lesson, I receive a message, *"1 Day Streak! Complete a lesson every day to build your streak!"* The app shows me one of five days complete. I can visually see my progress. As I stare at my screen, I notice a completed first day alongside four empty days, which triggers an innate desire to maintain my momentum and complete the next four days.

When a winning streak reaches a considerable length, it becomes even more precious to me. I do not want to lose my winning streak because I see the effort I have put in to reach that length. Therefore, I must progress every day to extend the winning streak. This leads to a winning streak that increases its attractiveness as it lengthens, becoming a self-reinforcing system.[89]

To help me along my journey, Duolingo makes use of the milestone technique, splitting larger tasks into smaller tasks. Streaks are popular in video games such as *Call of Duty, Cross Fire,* and *League of Legends.* While video games have proven the effectiveness of winning streaks, product design integrates little of this idea.

Streaks work. In fact, currently over seven hundred Duolingo users have an impressive streak longer than two

---

[89] Duy Huynh and Hiroyuki Iida, "An analysis of winning streak's effects in language course of "Duolingo."

thousand days. Streaks go from easy to hard, giving me a sense of quick progress. When I first begin, the streaks are easy to acquire, but as I continue using the app, the lessons become more challenging and so does keeping my streak alive.

The empty days Duolingo displays are intentional. It plays into our desire to reach perceived completion points, even if those completion points are entirely made up. Pseudo-set framing is arbitrarily grouping items or tasks as part of an apparent "set."[90] Drawing on Gestalt psychology, we tend to naturally categorize items as part of a set. Our minds perceive objects as part of a greater whole and as elements of a more complex system.[91] We see patterns where they don't exist—a phenomenon called "apophenia."[92] Pseudo-set framing leverages this phenomenon by arbitrarily grouping items or tasks as part of a set. This technique motivates users to reach perceived completion points. To put it simply, we don't like leaving things unfinished.

Pseudo-set framing satisfies our craving for a sense of progress. It enables us to feel progress in relation to specific reference points, even if those reference points are entirely made up. When working toward a larger goal, such as learning a new language, by framing action items as part of a set, our sense of progress is fulfilled by the incremental wins along the longer journey. This is the power of pseudo-sets. This strategy doesn't just break large tasks into small sets. It also provides a sense of completion along the journey and nudges us to continue until each set is complete.

---

90 Kate Barasz, et al, "Pseudo-set framing." 1460.
91 "What is Gestalt?"
92 Bruce Poulsen, "Being Amused by Apophenia."

On Duolingo, the grouping of these streaks is completely arbitrary. There was no reason why my next perceived completion point was in four days, but showing four empty days signaled to me that my next completion point was four days away, and boy was I motivated to get there. It was close enough that I could see myself achieving it, and I knew that when I did, I would feel a sense of progress. If it had been fifteen or twenty days, I might have said forget it. It's too far to achieve that goal. I'll never get there, so there doesn't seem to be a point in trying. For the time being, though, I am on a roll.

Three scientists—Gilovich, Vallone, and Tversky—had noticed something fascinating about basketball. There was this belief among players and fans about the idea of a "hot hand." If a player had sunk a few shots in a row in a relatively short period of time, players would keep feeding him or her the ball. The player had made so many previous shots in a row that they seemed more likely to make the next upcoming shot. A phenomenon called "the hot hand fallacy" (a.k.a., "the gambler's fallacy" or "the hot streak fallacy" or "the clustering illusion"), these researchers first published their findings in a 1985 edition of *Cognitive Psychology*. This fallacy was the idea that success feeds success.[93]

Nonetheless, when the researchers studied records of the Boston Celtics and Philadelphia '76ers making shots, they found that the "hot hand" was an illusion. A player's success on a previous shot slightly predicted they would miss the

---

93 Thomas Golovich, Robert Vallone, and Amos Tversky. "The hot hand in basketball: On the misperception of random sequences." 295-314.

subsequent shot, perhaps because the player was overconfident and would take riskier shots. The hot hand fallacy was all in their heads, but powerful, however, and one we all still fall prey to even though we know the science behind why it is false.[94]

The streaks in Duolingo have a similar effect. As you complete more lessons, you begin to feel you've built momentum. Since you've completed previous lessons, you're more likely to complete the next lesson. While Duolingo does not directly apply the "hot hand" fallacy, consistently completing a lesson provides the emotional experience of being "on a hot streak."

As I continued on my "hot streak," I noticed that the longer the chain became, the more difficult it was to break. Breaking it would mean starting all over, and all my hard work would go to waste. If I did break the chain, I might have just given up, which is how streaks can backfire. Just as one would stretch a rubber band, while pulling the rubber band provides a sense of fun, if that rubber band snaps, it's going to hurt, and you're not going to stretch another rubber band anytime soon.

Duolingo has countered this by allowing learners the ability to restore a broken streak. I notice that Duolingo grants me a gift in exchange for progress as one of my screens flashed, *"You've unlocked a gift! With this one-time streak freeze, you can miss one day of practice without losing your streak."*

Streaks are a powerful way to incentivize action. They provide a sense of progress that plays into the natural way we see the world, our desire to avoid loss, and our need for growth

---

94 Jamie Madigan, "Hot Hand Fallacy and Kill Streaks in Modern Warfare 2."

and accomplishment. While this technique is prominent in game design, product design fails to incorporate this powerful concept. This chapter has given you a glimpse into how products leverage the power of streaks. Now that you understand the psychological underpinnings of streaks, go create your own chain, but don't break it.

PART III:
BORN TO FOLLOW

CHAPTER 8:

THE CUES WE TAKE FROM OTHERS

"Mom, but all my friends are doing it. Why can't I?" I complained.

It was a beautiful final day of summer and the evening before my first day of eighth grade. In bed by 8:30 p.m. was the rule. My mom called me inside, interrupting the epic game of tag I was enjoying with my friends. I slammed the door behind me and begrudgingly walked up the steps. Hearing the laughter of my neighborhood friends through the upstairs windows made my curfew that much harder to follow. As I climbed into bed, I heard the echoes of fun and attempted to tune it all out with a local radio station.

I'd had enough. I got up out of bed, walked downstairs, and did what any eighth-grade boy would do when he didn't get his way. I complained. "It's so unfair! Why can't I play? Everyone else is allowed to stay out!" My mom's response, "If all your friends jumped off a bridge, would you?"

She had me, and I was stumped. I thought for a moment. Would I? It would seem stupid to jump off a bridge. Right?

I thought for a few more moments, and I concluded that yes, if all my friends were jumping off a bridge, I would follow them right over the edge.

My rationale was if all my friends were jumping off a bridge, the bridge wasn't dangerous. After all, why would everyone jump off a perfectly good bridge?

In the book *Influence: The Psychology of Persuasion*, psychologist Robert Cialdini states, "Whether the question is what to do with an empty popcorn box in a movie theater, how fast to drive on a certain stretch of highway, or how to eat the chicken at a dinner party, the actions of those around us will be important in defining the answer."[95]

Others give us cues regarding what we should do. Understanding what is and isn't acceptable based on the larger group is one of the most powerful influences that exists in our society. Others impact what we think, do and say—whether we realize it or not. We garner signals about what is acceptable and not acceptable based on the movement of the crowd regardless of whether the action is moral or right.[96]

Why do we follow the herd and adhere to social norms?

With limited information about what threats and dangers existed, our brains created shortcuts to determine what we needed to do to survive, and adhering to social norms was one of them. We observed what others were doing and used this as a signal of desirable behavior. These same mechanisms still drive much of our behavior today. "Keeping Up with the

---

95 Robert B. Cialdini, *Influence: The Psychology of Persuasion*.
96 Rob Henderson, "The Science Behind Why People Follow the Crowd."

Joneses" is a very real thing. This tendency dates back to the days of our ancestors.

As written in the book *The Elephant in the Brain,* foragers typically lived in groups of up to fifty individuals. Living a nomadic lifestyle, once resources at one location ran out, they would move to another location. Each person in the group relied heavily on the others for survival. While providing for themselves was a necessity, there was an unspoken contract between the group. When a member of the group was in need, the larger group would pitch in. If a member fell on hard times and couldn't provide for him or herself, the group was there to support them. To ensure that others would look out for you, you chipped in to help others in times of need. This was critical for your survival. To be without a band for an extended period was essentially a death sentence. You couldn't survive on your own. You needed the group.

One of the group's defining characteristics was its fierce egalitarianism. Members of the group, no matter how old or how young, were viewed as peers; there was no single leader. This structure prevented one individual from becoming too powerful and taking over the group. If a person became dominating or bullying, the group would ostracize that person. Ostracization could mean death since group membership was necessary for survival. The group had a way of managing itself, and any one leader was a threat to the group's long-term stability.[97]

---

[97] Kevin Simler and Robin Hanson. *The Elephant in the Brain: Hidden Motives in Everyday Life.*

Today, being ostracized from a group may not mean death, but we still carry these innate tendencies in our desire to belong, to fit in, to follow what everyone else is doing. Many of the common norms among our ancestors still exist today.

You may resist picking a fight with a person at work, not because you are worried about that person viewing you in a bad light, but because it could lead to your peers no longer including you in company functions. Picking a fight with a coworker could lead to others mistrusting you, which could then kick off a downward spiral where you underperform at your job, fall behind in your career, or even get fired. Social norms are powerful.

Our decisions regarding our behavior are primarily informed by what we observe from others. This is how we decide what is socially acceptable, appropriate, and popular. While this is an adaptive strategy in some regards, it can also lead to self-destructive behaviors that yield little to no benefit to us. We simply engage because that's what we see everyone else doing.

Herd behavior is making a decision based on the behavior of others, not necessarily your own preferences.[98] There is social pressure to conform because we want to be accepted. We behave in the same way as others, even if this behavior is immoral or not in our best interest. We assume the group is correct; the group knows something we don't.

We'll even follow the lead of people we don't know or have never met before.

---

98   James M. Russo, *Invest Like an Aardvark*.

In Robert Cialdini's book, *Influence*, he references an infamous California blackout.[99] To ensure this didn't happen again, the state of California wanted to encourage homeowners to conserve energy by reducing their A/C consumption and use fans instead. The question was how?

Researchers tested two approaches. One provided people with rational reasons to save energy, and the other tapped into our need to follow the herd. Researchers created two treatments in which they would go around to houses and hang door hangers with information to encourage homeowners to use less A/C. In the first treatment, the door hanger gave homeowners rational reasons for using less A/C—they could save the environment, it would help save them money, etc. In the second treatment, they referenced a majority percentage of their neighbors who were using fans instead of A/C.

The door hanger stating a rational reason for using fans instead of A/C did not impact A/C usage. Meanwhile, the other treatment that referenced the percentage of neighbors using fans instead of A/C showed a 6 percent decline in usage of A/C. This is a prime example of how individuals don't necessarily make optimal decisions in response to rational reasoning and how much influence others have on us, whether we know it or not.[100]

Even a small subset of a larger group making a confident move can influence the rest of the group.

Scientists at the University of Leeds instructed volunteers to randomly walk around a spacious hall without speaking to one another. A few of the volunteers were given specific directions in advance of where to walk. The walkers who

---

99 Robert B. Cialdini, Influence: *The Psychology of Persuasion*.
100 Wesley P. Schultz, et al, "The constructive, destructive, and reconstructive power of social norms." 429-434.

received specific directions influenced those who received no direction of where to walk. The key finding from this experiment was that it only takes about 5 percent of people who appear confident to influence the direction of the other 95 percent of the crowd. The best part was that the two hundred volunteers did this without even realizing it.[101]

While social norms can be used for evil, when leveraged strategically, they can help us do good. Whether assisting users in staying on track toward a fitness goal, sticking to a budget, or not giving up on learning a new skill, social norms employed correctly can be quite powerful.

Social norms and the pull of the crowd can help your users follow through on their intentions, an idea we'll explore in the following chapters. We'll explore how we learn to trust, what competition means for motivation, and why seemingly irrelevant bits of information about a group's members can have a significant impact on our decision to follow the crowd.

---

101 University of Leeds, "Sheep in Human Clothing: Scientists Reveal Our Flock Mentality."

CHAPTER 9:

MANUFACTURING A SOCIAL NORM

The elevator doors open, and inside stands a man in a trench coat, facing the elevator doors with his back to the rear of the elevator. A few seconds later, three additional people walk into the elevator and do something odd. Instead of turning and facing the same direction the other man, they stand face to face with him. Feeling a bit out of place and a tad confused as to why everyone else is facing him, he slowly turns around to face the same direction as the other three.

This scene ends and, moments later, a new scene begins.

The elevator door opens again, and inside is a man wearing a hat. He too has his back toward the rear of the elevator, facing the elevator doors. Shortly after, three men walk into the elevator and stand face to face with this man. The man turns around to face the back of the elevator, conforming to the direction of the others. The doors close.

Moments later, the doors open, and all four men are now facing sideways. Although I could not see what happened while the doors were closed, I assumed three of the men turned sideways and the fourth followed suit.

The stunt, entitled "Face the Rear," was a prank from an episode of *Candid Camera* that aired in 1962. An elevator door would open and in would walk a few people who were all in on the joke. They would face in the opposite direction of the person in the elevator in the hopes that the person would simply follow what they were doing without reason.

In both instances, each individual followed the norm of the group without being provided context or a reason. Originally standing in one direction, when the group moved, so did the individual.[102] The power of the group is a strong force. When everyone is taking action, we assume there is a good reason, and we will often follow along without questioning why.

Social psychologists have been studying the human tendency to act as part of a group since at least the nineteenth century. Our tendency to follow social norms is present in our behavior and interactions. We want to make socially desirable decisions, so we are attuned to what other people are doing, i.e., keeping up with the Joneses.[103]

Information about others' behavior is enough to influence us. We don't have to physically see people behaving in a certain way. This phenomenon, combined with our sensitivity to the way information is framed, makes it easy to

---

102 Ayun Halliday, "The Power of Conformity: 1962 Episode of Candid Camera Reveals the Strange Psychology of Riding Elevators."
103 Nate Andorsky, "5 Behavioral Economics Theories To Keep Your Nonprofit From Getting Left Behind – Creative Science."

communicate social information to override initial inclinations. This is also one of the reasons why the "Only four left!" notification when online shopping can be such a powerful mechanism for convincing buyers. It implicitly communicates that everyone else has already bought this product, and creates a sense of urgency because soon you won't be able to follow the crowd once the last few run out.[104,105] Social norms are a powerful force and, if leveraged correctly, can nudge users to take the actions that are in their best interest and interests of the group.

Danvers Fluery started Talented to help people learn new skills. Talented was driven by the belief that to learn a new skill, one needs to put newly acquired knowledge into practice immediately. To address this, Danvers built a new type of learning platform.

He borrowed the core concept from the apprenticeship model that came to be during the later Middle Ages, a time when life didn't extend beyond a couple of square miles for most people. Their knowledge of the world at large was limited compared to what we know today, but there was a proven path to skill development through apprenticeships. Upon choosing a trade, an apprentice would work under the direction of a master, learning the skills and techniques of his trade until he was ready to go off on his own.

This method of skill development, also known as work-based learning experiences, allows the opportunity for the

---

104 Robert B. Cialdini, Influence: *The Psychology of Persuasion*.
105 Rob Henderson, "The Science Behind Why People Follow the Crowd."

mentor to provide direct feedback to the mentee. It allows learners to remove themselves from a classroom setting and apply their knowledge through hands-on training. Additionally, this allows the application of a newly learned skill in a real environment to further reinforce learning.

In the last century, much of this began to change. For the first time in human history, information was distributed on a mass scale. With the rise of inventions such as the printing press, the television, and computers came a change in the way we learn.

With the ability to distribute knowledge on a mass scale, the thought was that learning and skill development would rapidly improve too. No longer were teachers bound to a one-to-one model. Rather it could be one-to-many, one to even millions. Nonetheless, users were learning new skills, but these users weren't putting their skills into practice. With the democratization of learning, we consequently drained the one-to-one interaction that was so powerful.

When Danvers started Talented, their hypothesis was simple. People weren't using new skills at work because they weren't learning them. He proposed that if they learned them, they would start using them. "Our thought was, if you give them the opportunity to learn skills, they will take advantage of it," said Danvers.

Danvers adds, "People are trying to develop skills by listening and watching videos and hoping it will happen by osmosis, but this typically doesn't work." Knowing this, Danvers set out on a mission to create a platform that not only helped individuals learn but motivated them to put their newfound skills into practice.

Talented is more than just a technology platform. As stated on the Talented website, *"This success is born from modern neuroscientific research, applied behavioral economics and a walloping dose of common sense."*[106]

The software blends learning with proven, time-honored skill development methods such as the apprenticeship model to help people become better leaders, better managers, and better teachers. Employers offer the platform to their employees to help them learn skills such as resilience, values-based leadership, and managing ambiguity. By dedicating as little as five to ten minutes a day, employees learn new skills and have the opportunity to put their new skills to work.

Danvers and his team borrowed from a large body of neuroscientific research and built a product that encourages people to learn but, more importantly, put their new skills to use. The software is intent on not only educating its users but also assigning them "missions" to go out to practice and prove their skill mastery in the real world. They measure their success based how many users are applying their new skills in their day-to-day work.

After launching, Danvers quickly ran into a problem. Users were consuming the educational material, but they weren't using their skills. Their team had nailed the learning part; they had created an experience that was easy to use and made it simple for employees to gain access to content and learn new skills.

Still, metrics were telling the same story. Users were supposed to implement their newly acquired skills and then upload real-life evidence—images, video, audio, and text of their practice to be assessed by the Talented staff—but this wasn't happening. Users were learning, but they weren't using their newly acquired skills.

---

106 "Talented."

After all, this was the ultimate goal that Talented set out to achieve. Without this, Talented was a failure. What good was it if users weren't using their new skills? The Talented team was stumped, what could be happening? They began trying various tactics to solve this problem.

What if his team rewarded users for completing these five- to ten-minute lessons? The team incorporated a system of rewards to encourage users to use their skills, testing various models to increase uptake. Theoretically, it sounded like a good idea, but it backfired.

After offering $5 gift cards to users for completing microcourses, something interesting happened. It triggered what is known as mental accounting. Equating their time with money, users assumed that their ten to fifteen minutes spent on the software completing a lesson was worth $5. Providing compensation in this way was problematic. The more Talented wanted their users to use the platform, the more they would have to compensate them. Furthermore, it was triggering extrinsic motivation, whereas the Talented team wanted to trigger intrinsic motivation.

To counter this effect, they realized that a $.50 donation based on achieving specific benchmarks as a group was a more effective way to motivate users. "We'd take a group of learners, maybe a hundred people within an organization, and we'd say, 'Hey, we're going to make a charitable donation on behalf of your group that is going to increase depending on your level of participation.'"

With these approaches, they saw the numbers move a bit, but they were still concerned about the long-term viability of the company.

The team reached a point where if they didn't pivot, Talented would go out of business. Stuck at a dead end and out of ideas, they didn't know where to turn. At this point, they dug into the academic literature to first understand what the issue was and then to determine a behavioral-first solution.

Their initial faulty assumption was a common one: give people access to the information they need, and they'll put it to good use. The approach seemed logical; people make poor decisions because they don't have access to the right information. Give them better access to information, and their behavior will change.

At that time they met Dan Ariely, who leads Duke University's Startup Lab, which helps startups incorporate behavioral science into their products. This meeting became a crucial turning point in Danvers' and Talented's journey. Dan's lab helped the Talented team understand they were indeed tackling the wrong problem.

Knowledge and access to educational content is a stage-gate to behavioral change, but it was in no way predictive of behavior change. Providing access to educational content would not drive engagement. The solution—come up with an idea that drove behavior change.

Danvers added, "What we're dealing with had to do with motivation and engagement, and Dan Ariely knew that cold. This was the inflection point of our business going from just another learning platform to something interesting." Epiphany. Talented isn't in the learning business after all. They are in the business of changing people's environments.

"The way to drive behavioral change predicatively is by changing norms and changing the rules, effectively changing someone's environment," said Danvers.

The question then became how to drive this behavior. The solution to drive behavioral change is to shift the norms and change the rules. Working with Dan's team, Danvers understood what theories to implement to change behavior. Armed with this knowledge, their team tested approaches and found success in one—the use of cohorts.

Talented places users into a small group providing them access to the progress of other students in their cohort. This creates a social norm for how the group should be progressing through the content. Each week, the group receives a notification about how the rest of their cohort is progressing.

Danvers said, "When a user signs up, everyone has three weeks to finish their course. Typically, by day three or four, you have a few true believers who are ahead of the pack and off to a fast start."

They send a simple message to the entire group, congratulating those few in the group who are off to a quick start. For example, a message to the group would read, "Congratulations, John, you just hit the bronze reward tier! Keep it up!"

This message wasn't a shame gram, punishing learners for falling behind. It was merely insight into how the rest of the cohort was progressing. The early learners set the social norm for the group, and those who had yet to start began to change their behavior. They saw the movement of the group as the norm and felt compelled to conform. Danvers saw a massive uptick in engagement from implementing this behavioral-first approach.

Knowing this same approach is used in game design, Danvers explored online gaming models for hints on how to optimize his cohorts. Valued at over 33 billion US dollars, online gaming models hold a wealth of knowledge on how to motivate users.[107] He found that fifty was a successful number of people for a cohort.

---

107 Christina Gough, "US Online Gaming Industry—Statistics & Facts."

With this new shift, Talented saw success that not even their competitors were experiencing. Their metrics backed it up. Eighty percent of people who practiced on Talented went on to use the skill at work within one hour of learning it. Typical online learning platforms are lucky to see a 5 percent conversion on this metric.

When incorporating a behavioral-first approach into a product, Danvers discovered that you need a combination of many behavioral science ideas to achieve success. One of the critical insights to Danvers' solution was understanding the behavior to shift, not the outcome. Once they focused in on this, the puzzle pieces started to come together. Understand how to change the behavior, and the outcome will follow. As Danvers learned, keeping up with the pack can be a powerful motivator. After all, no one wants to be left behind.

CHAPTER 10:

SIGNALS OF TRUST

In 1992, Disney released what would become one of its most iconic films—*Aladdin*. The story chronicles a poor street urchin, Aladdin, who spends his time stealing food from the marketplace in the city of Agrabah. One day he happens to meet a young Princess by the name of Jasmine, whose father is forcing her to wed.[108]

Aladdin's luck takes a turn for the better when he retrieves a magical lamp from the Cave of Wonders with a genie that will grant him three wishes. The genie informs him that he can grant almost any wish, but he can't kill, raise the dead, or make people fall in love.

With the hope of winning Princess Jasmine's love, Aladdin asks the Genie to turn him into a prince. One of the most memorable scenes from the film is the infamous magic carpet ride. Dressed as a prince, Aladdin, pining for Jasmine's love, swoops in during the middle of the night on a flying carpet in an attempt to impress his crush.

As he approaches on his flying carpet, she asks him, "How are you doing that?"

---

108 Aladdin, directed by Ron Clements and John Musker.

"It's a magic carpet. It's lovely. You don't, uh, you don't want to go for a ride, do you? We could get out of the palace, see the world," replies Aladdin.

A look of hesitation can be seen on Jasmine's face as she begins to debate internally whether this would be a good idea.

"Is it safe?" she replies.

"Sure. Do you trust me?" Aladdin replies.

"What?" Jasmine replies with a hint of hesitation in her voice.

"Do you trust me..." Aladdin responds.

After a brief pause, she replies, "Yes."

She steps onto the magic carpet and the iconic song, "A Whole New World," plays as the magic carpet takes Jasmine and Aladdin through the land of Egypt, speeding through the foothills and flying above the ancient pyramids.

Romantic, right? Boy meets girl; he asks her to take a risk with him, and off they go into the sunset, falling in love. Would you jump onto a flying carpet with a guy or girl you barely knew? To who knows where?

Think about this for a second. A guy, pining for your love, whom you don't know at all, asks you to get on an object that you've never before seen in your life. He is going to fly you through the air, and you have idea of where you two are going, what's going to happen on the trip, or when or if you'll come back. Your mother would be furious.

And you say yes.

Why did Jasmine decide to trust Aladdin? What about him gave her a sense of security? Even though the logical side of her brain said it wasn't a good idea, why did her emotional side override it and convince her to take the leap of faith?

What factors influence the likelihood that we'll trust someone enough to jump on that magic carpet? To decide to take the risk and believe the action you're about to take is safe? To follow others and, even without knowing them, have blind faith that their ideas or actions are indicative of what you should do?

When the logical side of the brain seems to slow down, similarity bias may very well take over. We have a natural inclination to trust people who look and act like us. We tend to befriend and marry people who resemble ourselves. Adam Hampton, Amanda Fisher Boyd, and Susan Sprecher propose several different reasons for this in a study published in *The Journal of Social and Personal Relationships*.[109,110]

A few factors can accentuate the extent to which we inform our behavior based on a particular individual. The first is similarity—if we perceive an individual to be like ourselves across some dimension (e.g., gender, race, favorite sports team, etc.), we feel closer and more attracted to that person. Hence, we are more likely to look to their decisions to inform our own.[111]

Consensual validation, meeting people who share our attitudes, makes us feel more confident in our own beliefs about the world. Jasmine was from royalty, so she is more comfortable trusting Aladdin, who she assumes to be royalty as well.

Given that she has just met Aladdin, there is much information about him that she does not know, but she begins, as

---

[109] Gwendolyn Seidman, "Why Do We Like People Who Are Similar to Us?"
[110] Adam J. Hampton, Amanda N. Fisher Boyd, and Susan Sprecher, "You're like me and I like you: Mediators of the similarity–liking link assessed before and after a getting-acquainted social interaction." 2221-2244.
[111] "Similarity/Attraction Theory."

we all do, to fill in the unknown information based on her own experiences. Even though she doesn't know for sure, she assumes Aladdin goes to fancy events, eats lavish food, and has servants because that is the way she lives. She then believes Aladdin, like her, has other positive characteristics even if she hasn't seen them yet. She extrapolates what Aladdin *should* be like based on what she knows about others in his royal "group."

We also assume someone who has a much in common with us is more likely to like us. After all, we want others to like us, and when spending time with someone similar to us, the certainty of being liked increases. We assume the more we have in common with that person, the higher the likelihood they will like us is.

By jumping on this carpet with Aladdin, Jasmine explores a new world while psychologically minimizing the risk of doing so. According to self-expansion theory, one benefit of relationships is that we can gain new knowledge and experiences by spending time with someone else. Theoretically, a dissimilar person is more likely to provide new knowledge and experiences to us, so we should seek out people who are very different from us to acquire new knowledge and experiences.

However, this isn't what we do. Research shows we are more likely to seek self-expansion opportunities when interacting with someone similar, rather than dissimilar, allowing us to expand our horizons while also feeling safe. Jumping onto a magic carpet into a Whole New World was the perfect opportunity for Jasmine to safely gain new experiences, given that it's with someone she perceives to be similar to herself.

Airbnb discovered this when they were in the early stages of building their business. Airbnb is an online marketplace that connects people who want to rent out their homes with people who are looking for a place to stay. They do not own any real estate listings and they function as a broker, receiving commissions from each booking.[112]

A revolutionary concept, many considered it crazy—asking strangers to open their homes to strangers.

Airbnb is now a worldwide brand name and has built up a considerable amount of trust equity as a company, but to get there, they had to overcome a significant hurdle—getting strangers to trust one another.

Airbnb was rejected by several investors who could have had 10 percent of the company for $150,000 in 2008, with some citing the model wouldn't work because strangers would never let other strangers into their homes.[113]

Your home is one of your most personal possessions. It is a direct reflection of who you are as a person. Walk into a person's home, and you garner what type of person they are within minutes by the way their home is decorated.

Asking a host to open a home to random strangers is quite personal, so the question becomes: how do you get people to open one of their most intimate environments to strangers?

"We were aiming to build Olympic trust between people that had never met," said Joe Gebbia, a cofounder and former Chief Product Officer of Airbnb, on his *TED* Talk.[114]

---

112 Jean Folger, "Airbnb: Advantages and Disadvantages."
113 Alexei Oreskovic, "Airbnb was rejected by seven investors who could have had 10 percent of the company for $150,000 in 2008."
114 Joe Gebbia, "How Airbnb designs for trust."

One way to garner trust is through a review system, but this only works at scale. If a listing has positive reviews, prospective renters are more likely to stay at the home, but no one wants the be the guinea pig. How can you encourage a renter to book a property that has little to no reviews?

It's a chicken and the egg problem. If there is a new listing on the website without any reviews, no one wants to stay at the home, but without getting people to stay at the home, there will be no one to leave reviews. Same for renters. If a renter has zero reviews about how good of a tenant they are, no one will want to rent to them. How can you jumpstart this process? How can you build trust between two people who have never met before in the absence of multiple reviews?

Create similarity between the renter and rentee.

You can manufacture trust by exposing the right amount of information to the right types of people in the right way. Airbnb conducted a joint study with Stanford and found that two people's similarity in age, geographic location, etc. correlated to an increase in willingness to rent to one another. The more two people resembled each other, the more likely they were to trust each other.[115]

We saw the same phenomenon in Aladdin's interaction with Jasmine. We prefer people who are like us—the more someone is like us, the more likely we are to trust them. The more different they are, the less we trust them.

During his *TED* Talk, Joe also mentioned that if you share too little or too much about yourself, acceptance rates go down. If it's too impersonal, just saying "Yo," or too

---

[115] Bruno Abrahao, et al, "Reputation offsets trust judgments based on social biases among Airbnb users." 9848-9853.

much, "I am having issues with my mother," acceptance rates go down. But one zone is just right. For example, "Love the artwork in your place, coming for vacation from my family."[116]

So how did they design for this? Airbnb nudged users to write an introduction of the correct length and to include the right details about themselves.

We have a natural tendency to fill what's empty. The size of the input box where you introduce yourself is intentionally a specific size, giving the user guardrails for how much information he or she should share. Also prompts guide the user, such as:

> *Tell Susan a little bit about yourself.*
> *What brings you to Atlanta?*
> *Who's joining you?*
> *What do you love about this listing?*

Airbnb discovered that at a certain point, reviews trumped similarity bias. When a listing accumulated more than ten reviews, everything changed. After ten reviews, a high reputation overcomes the similarity bias. The greater Airbnb community now validated the host, and this was enough to overcome the similarity bias. However, without integrating similarity bias, many of the listings would have never been able to reach the ten-review mark.

"It turns out, a well-designed reputation system is key for building trust, and we didn't get it right the first time," said Joe as he wrapped up his *TED* Talk.

---

116 Joe Gebbia, "How Airbnb designs for trust."

We derive much of what we believe to be safe and true from what those around us believe to be safe and true. Making social comparisons related to demographic information can increase the effect of similarity bias. If your product has a component that allows your users to interact with other users, show them how similar they are to one another.

CHAPTER 11:

NEVER OUT OF THE GAME

"What? How did you win? I was in first the whole time, and you were in last! What happened?" I said to my sister Lilly as we wrapped up an intense game of *Mario Kart* with our cousins.

She was Peach, and I was Mario. She was in last place the entire race as I led by a hefty margin. As we came to the final lap, she was hot on my tail, acquiring all types of weapons such as mushrooms, bananas, and boosters. As I am seconds from crossing the finish line, bam. She shoots a turtle shell for a direct hit, sending my cart in the air, twirling round and round. Lilly zooms past me to take first place and win the race.

Playing video games isn't how I spend most of my time, but I do enjoy a great game of *Mario Kart*. Growing up, my family and I traveled to see my cousins and grandparents in Florida. Of course, I was excited to see my aunt, uncle, grandparents, and cousins, but I was even more excited about the great games of *Mario Kart* that were to be battled in due time.

After spending time visiting with the family, we would huddle into my cousins' living room, grab controllers, and plop down in front of their large screen TV. After arguing back and forth about who got to be Mario, we'd pick our players and were off to the races, literally. There were five of us but only four controllers, so the rule was that whoever came in last had to give up their controller for the next race.

If you aren't familiar with *Mario Kart*, it is a simple and entertaining game, a series of go-kart-style racing video games developed and published by Nintendo. For those who have played, you know how addicting the game can be. Players race around a track on go-karts, grabbing weapons and firing them at competing players. For example, you can pick up a banana peel and hold onto it until a player is behind you and then place it on the track and watch them slip on it.

We weren't paid to play or compensated in any way, but we would keep going for hours on end. What about this activity kept us so engaged? To get an idea, let's look at redwood trees.

A few years ago, I visited the redwood trees in Muir Woods in California with some of my college buddies. Trekking along the cold, foggy trail, we stood in amazement at what we saw. Having grown up on the east coast, I had only seen trees that were maybe two stories tall. I had seen pictures of famous redwood trees, but those photos didn't do them justice.

As I turned my head upward, I stood in amazement. These trees were dozens of stories tall, so tall that it was difficult to see the top of them. Our walk gave me a snapshot in time of a competition centuries in the making between these trees. Each tree was inching taller than the ones beside it in a fight for survival. If a tree didn't grow tall enough, it meant death.

Natural selection means that winners survive, losers cease to exist. Redwood trees are trapped in this endless cycle of competition, as Robin Hanson explains in his book, *The Elephant in the Brain*. "It takes a lot of energy for redwood trees to grow as large as they are. There is evidence of redwoods reaching as tall as four hundred feet and beyond. For context, four hundred feet is equivalent to forty to fifty stories."[117]

But why bother? Why do these trees put so much effort into growth? The trees are locked in an arms race to get the most sunlight. To survive, each tree needs sunlight, and the surest way to get sunlight is to be the tallest tree. Without height, the trees die.

A tree grows tall only because all the other trees surrounding it grow tall, but this process is wasteful. If all the trees coordinated and did not grow beyond, let's say, five feet, they would all have access to sunlight and not waste energy growing forty stories tall. The redwood trees are more towering than they need to be, but they can't coordinate, so natural selection takes over. The same drive that pushes redwoods to grow moves us to compete, and competition can be a powerful force to nudge users to take action.

During the chapter on streaks, we looked at how a language learning app was leveraging behavioral science. Duolingo's success is no accident; their team has gamified the entire learning experience. Users can earn badges, progress through levels, and compete against other learners.

---

[117] Kevin Simler and Robin Hanson. *The Elephant in the Brain: Hidden Motives in Everyday Life.*

Sean Chin, a designer at Duolingo, phrases it this way, "At the end of the day, we're trying to encourage people to do something that's intrinsically difficult. Learning a language is not easy. That's why we have to introduce all these mechanics to incentivize learning."[118]

After signing up for the app, I complete my first ten lessons shortly thereafter. Duolingo then places me in a cohort with a group of fifty other players. My cohort is comprised of people who completed their first lesson around the same time as I did, placing me against others who are at relatively the same place as me. I have access to a leaderboard, which enables me to see where I stand against others in my cohort at any given moment.

Each user in my cohort has an avatar, a cartoon type of character meant to represent the user. I am not able to physically see others in my cohort, but these avatars provide me with a sense that I am indeed competing with real individuals.

Each cohort of fifty is part of a league, such as the Amethyst League or the Ruby League. I can visually see at the top of the screen the various leagues. As soon as I move into the top ten, I see a nice green text appear: "Promotion Zone." This zone creates a visual incentive to work hard to ensure I don't fall out of the "Promotion Zone." Moving from tenth to eleventh no longer feels like falling by one spot, it feels like a much larger setback.

Similar to the Redwood trees, I too am trapped in a cycle of competition. Now that I have clear insight into how other are progressing compared to me, my competitive nature kicks in. I find myself constantly checking my app,

---

118 Jordan Koschei, "How Duolingo Designs with Psychology in Mind."

ensuring I am progressing against my cohort members. I am determined to make it to the next league and leave my competition behind.

Leaderboards spur competition, but they have weaknesses. Leaderboards can backfire. If a user gets too far ahead or too far behind, they disengage. If you get stuck in last place and feel it's impossible to catch up, it becomes easy to rationalize giving up. The design of *Mario Kart* has a fascinating feature to counter this problem.

One feature of *Mario Kart* is the use of various power-up items players can grab by driving into item boxes laid out on the course. These power-ups include mushrooms to give players a speed boost, Koopa Shells to be thrown at opponents, banana peels, and explosive boxes that can be laid on the course as hazards. Players' current positions influence the type of weapons they can grab in the race. Players lagging far behind may receive more powerful items while the leader may receive small defensive items. They can also perform driving techniques during the race, such as mini-turbos, slipstreaming, and rocket starts.

A popular feature in game design to increase engagement and retention, Dynamic game difficulty balancing (DGDB), also known as dynamic difficulty adjustment (DDA) or dynamic game balancing (DGB), is the process of automatically changing parameters, scenarios, and behaviors in a video game in real-time based on the player's ability, to avoid making the player bored (if the game is too easy) or frustrated (if it is too hard). Often referred to as rubber banding, this gameplay mechanism allows other players a realistic chance to catch up to the leading player. The idea is to keep the player engaged by letting them know they are never permanently in first or last.[119]

While rubber banding is relatively apparent in *Mario Kart*, as you play, you subconsciously begin to learn that you are never truly out of the game. You understand that no matter how far behind you are, you are a few seconds away from grabbing a power-up that can propel you into first place. Furthermore, if you are in first, that doesn't mean you'll stay there long.

Duolingo leverages this approach, ensuring users don't fall too far behind the group or get too far ahead.

A leaderboard cycle currently runs from Monday to Sunday, and each week, Duolingo pairs me with fifty new users. If I am in the top ten by week's end, I am "promoted" to a higher league. Dynamically adjusting my league ensures I am always competing against other users who are within the same activity range as me. If I fall into the bottom five of any league, I am placed back to a less competitive league.[120] Effectively, Duolingo is using the same game-balancing technique as Mario Kart by shifting me in and out of groups based on my relative performance.

Duolingo has taken another page out of *Mario Kart* by offering power-ups that allow me to catch up if I fall behind. I am able to earn gems, which I can use to buy items from Duolingo's shop. These items help me "catch-up" or "fix a mistake" if I find myself falling behind. That include items such as:

---

119 Lizeth Joseline Fuentes Pérez et al., "Dynamic Game Difficulty Balancing in Real Time Using Evolutionary Fuzzy Cognitive Maps."
120 HelpfulDuo, "Leaderboards now on all Android devices (updated)."

"Double or Nothing—Double your fifty gem wager by maintaining a seven-day streak."

"Streak Freeze—Streak Freeze allows your streak to remain in place for one full day of inactivity."

There are various ways to utilize rubber banding in product design, and Barry Fishman has built a successful software product with this technique in mind. Barry Fishman is an Arthur F. Thurnau Professor of Learning Technologies at the University of Michigan School of Information and School of Education. Barry is at the cutting edge of reimagining how students are educated to make learning more enjoyable. To understand the impact of Barry's creation, let's take a stroll around campus.

Imagine it's your first day of college, the sun is shining, students are abuzz on campus. You grab your morning coffee and head to your first class of the semester. As you enter the large building at the center of campus and walk toward room 202, you can feel the first day jitters in your stomach. You swing the door open and proceed to the large lecture hall, consisting of almost two hundred students. After grabbing your seat, you place your backpack down and open your laptop.

The professor begins the class, "Welcome to Econ 101. Unlike most professors, I run things a bit differently here. In my class, to achieve a grade, you'll acquire points. Every student starts with zero points today. To earn an A, you'll need to earn at least ten thousand points throughout the semester. There are multiple ways to earn points. Please check your email. You have received a link to a platform we are using—Gradecraft."

Gradecraft is a learning management software that enables educators to build game courses for their students. The idea is, if you give educators the tools to turn their existing courses into a game, students will be eager to play and will enjoy learning rather than dread it.

"The tagline for our work is that school is a game, but it's a terrible game with all the wrong incentive systems. In most schools, students are primarily focused on the grade. We're trying to design the system so that students are focused on the learning, and good grades are the outcome of good learning," notes Barry.

The product's homepage explains the approach the platform is built on, stating, "Gameful learning is a pedagogical approach inspired by techniques and methods found in well-designed games." Gameful pedagogy means building game elements in the design of the actual educational course, rather than just adding gamification techniques to an existing course.

You check your inbox and open the email, click the link and log on to the website.

The software incorporates four main concepts. Earning up: all students start with zero points and earn their way up as they complete certain milestones and activities. Increase autonomy: empowering students to decide when and what type of assignments they would like to do. The freedom to fail: if a student scores poorly on an assignment, they can always make up the points by completing a different assignment. And tangible progress: students can see their progress at any time, unlock levels and badges, and see how they are progressing against their peers if they opt into the leaderboard.

The tactics used by Gradecraft are borrowed directly from game design. As their website states, many of their game design principles apply what they have learned from Self-determination Theory about building intrinsic motivation. People want to be able to have control over their choices, be challenged, and feel connected to those around them.

Contrary to how *Mario Kart* is structured, Barry has found that in a learning environment, "Competition works best as a motivator when it's not a winner take all. The idea that there will be winners and losers at the end of the learning experience is problematic."

Yet, Gradecraft still leverages competition in a unique way. Rather than pitting students against one another, Barry encourages groups of students to motivate each other toward achieving a group goal.

He adds, "I use competition to entice them to be engaged. I am against leaderboards in general because I am against ranking students. With a leaderboard, from your point of view, there are three people: you, the person above you, and the person behind you."

In one of his current courses, he split the students into eight teams of ten students, and each team is competing against one another to hit certain milestones and benchmarks. Rather than pitting students against one another, this encourages a team approach where groups of students compete against other groups of students.

The professor continues, "Throughout the semester, you can earn points for various activities: scoring high on a test, doing well on a paper, turning in homework, completing a learning activity, etc. Furthermore, if you mess up on an assignment, or do poorly on a test, you'll have the chance to make it up."

This point system encourages teachers to set up their courses to give students the freedom to fail. With the freedom to fail, students have the freedom to take risks. Students push themselves outside of their comfort zone and select assignments that challenge them beyond their normal limits because if they fail, there is a way to catch up.

If a student needs ten thousand points to earn an A in a course, the instructor may make it possible to acquire twelve thousand points so if a student does poorly on an assignment, they can make up the difference. Each student has access to their own grade prediction tool, essentially allowing students to chart out which activities and milestones they need to hit to acquire the number of points they want.

This point system is a unique way of integrating rubber banding. The platform's grade prediction tool allows students to chart their path to success. Barry notes, "We provide multiple pathways for the student to get to their end goal."

As I wrapped up my call with Barry, he mentioned a story that demonstrates the power of his system. He recalled a conversation with a young woman a few years ago who came to him in distress; she explained she was out sick for some time and wasn't able to complete one of the larger assignments for the class. Since she was so far behind, she had given up on the course because, in her mind, it was impossible for her to catch up.

Barry pulled up the grade predictor tool, turned the computer for her to see, and showed her multiple paths she could take and still receive a good grade in the class. After realizing this, she responded, "Wow, I feel motivated to do this now."

Barry had done something simple yet powerful to trigger motivation; he let her know that, contrary to what she thought, she wasn't out of the game. Barry's approach seems to be working. As of the summer of 2019, his platform is used across seventy-four academic institutions, and more than sixteen thousand students have engaged with the product.

Competition between users is a powerful technique to motivate action, but as you can see, it is not one size fits all. While one approach may work in one context, in other settings, it may have adverse side effects. It could create an environment that is counterproductive to the goals of your users. While we're hard-wired to compete, it is critical to employ mechanisms, such as the ones Barry has, where players feel like they are never out of the game.

PART IV:
HOW WE DECIDE

CHAPTER 12:

DECISIONS, DECISIONS

Olympic gymnasts begin training at a very young age and dedicate their entire lives to their craft. Talent isn't enough to propel them to the top of their game; it takes hard work and dedication.

"When I was younger," McKayla said, "I would be watching *Tarzan* and running around on all fours. My mom was like, 'I need to put this child in gymnastics. She's crazy.' I was technically in gymnastics at the age of two and always felt comfortable in the gym."[121]

It's August 5, 2012, at the London Olympics, and McKayla Maroney, a member of the women's US gymnastics team, is about to receive a medal for her accomplishments. As McKayla is waiting to receive her Olympic medal, the soundtrack to *Chariots of Fire* fills the stadium. Dreaming of this moment all her life, she finally reached the pinnacle of her career, or so it seemed.

McKayla is called to receive her medal. Waving to the crowd, she steps up to the podium and leans over as the official places the medal around her neck. McKayla is doing her

---

121 Zara Humphrey, "McKayla Maroney Opens Up On Her Life As An Olympian."

best to keep a straight, happy face, but as the camera pans to her, she seems annoyed, pissed off, even a bit unamused. An expression of "not impressed" is written all over her face, and the crowd does not fail to notice. Within days, the iconic image of her face goes viral, dubbed the "not impressed face."

McKayla had won a silver medal during the 2012 London Olympics, an achievement many of us could only dream of. How could she not smile after being recognized as one of the world's greatest athletes? In her mind, she didn't win silver. She lost the gold.

The choices we make don't happen in a vacuum. While McKayla's experience of competing in the Olympics is not something most of us can relate to, many of us can understand the emotional experience of working toward a goal and coming up short.[122]

Every day we strive to make sense of the environment around us, and we make decisions that are heavily impacted by reference points. The information we know and see can cloud the choices we make, for better or worse. A loss may be a loss in one context, but in another, it may be a win. A promotion feels great but may feel even better if you are one of the few who received it.

Think about your last trip to a grocery store; perhaps milk was all you needed. You planned to make a quick trip, grab

---

122 Laurie Santos and Michelle Kwan, "Episode 3: A Silver Lining." 40:34.

milk, and be home before dinner time. But as you walk out of the store, you find yourself leaving with not only milk, but also a bag of chips, a few candy bars, and a couple of boxes of cereal.

Logically, it would make sense to place the most frequently purchased products in a "quick grab items" section of the grocery right as you walk in. The most commonly purchased items should be easily accessible so customers can get in and out as quickly as possible.

Oddly enough, I have yet to come across a grocery store that has a quick-grab section. Instead, items such as milk, bread, and eggs are at the back of the market. On an episode of *Planet Money*, Michael Pollen notes, "My general impression is that the milk is in the back, but it's also usually very far from the bread. Both of them are very common items, and so it makes you cover a lot of ground if you want them."[123]

Store designers construct these pathways intentionally. While designers understand users have free will, they also know the presentation of items in a grocery store influences what consumers choose to purchase. Similar to McKayla's experience, where her silver medal seemed subpar next to her dreams of the gold, a $20 bottle of wine at a grocery store may look cheap, but only next to a $75 bottle of wine. Remove the $75 bottle of wine and place it next to a $15 bottle of wine, and suddenly the $20 bottle of wine doesn't look as cheap.[124]

Walk down another aisle and see a jar of ice cream labeled "80 percent fat-free," and you'll stop to purchase

---

123 David Kestenbaum, "Everyone Goes To The Store To Get Milk. So Why's It Way In The Back?" 4:27.
124 Amos Tversky and Daniel Kahneman, "Loss aversion in riskless choice: A reference-dependent model." 1039-1061.

this calorie-saving treat. In that same aisle, you see a jar of ice cream labeled "20 percent fat," and you'll continue shopping. Both jars of ice cream contain the same amount of fat, but merely changing the framing of the label can influence your willingness to buy.

You turn toward the chip aisle and grab a few bags of Doritos, but you fail to notice the Tostitos placed below eye level. Swap the bags and place the Tostitos at eye level, and sales of Tostitos increase. As you purchase these chips, you're consciously unaware of the conversation you had with your buddy yesterday about whether Cool Ranch or Nacho Doritos are better. Still, unbeknownst to you, this had a priming effect on your purchasing preference. In the absence of this conversation, you may not have bought those bags of chips.

As you continue to walk through the store, you can't help but notice the endless options: twenty different types of salad dressings, forty different pasta sauces, and fifteen different types of peanut butter. You feel overwhelmed. The way options are presented greatly influences our decisions. All these items in the store occupy space and their arrangement, the Choice Architecture, impacts our decision-making.[125]

In 2004, Barry Schwartz, an American psychologist, published a book titled *The Paradox of Choice–Why Less Is More*. His thesis rests on a basic concept: as humans, we want freedom, and freedom means access to endless options. However,

---

[125] Richard Thaler and Cass Sunstein, *Nudge*.

Barry Schwartz discovered that when presented with too many options, we have a hard time making a decision.[126]

In a paramount jam study in 2000, psychologists Sheena Iyengar and Mark Lepper published a remarkable study uncovering the truth behind this.[127] One day at a supermarket, shoppers saw twenty-four different types of jam. Those who sampled the jam received a coupon for $1 off their purchase of any of the twenty-four jams. On a different day, shoppers passed the same table, but this time, there were only six different types of jam.

When twenty-four different types of jam were displayed, more people stopped, but only 6 percent purchased. Conversely, when the number of jams presented narrowed to six, the purchase rate went up drastically, but fewer people stopped to look at jams. It seemed that when there were twenty-four different types of jams, shoppers fell into analysis paralysis; there were so many options that the thought of having to decide became too daunting.

Presenting users with too many options can create a cognitive overload. There are too many decisions to compare and contrast, so we decide the easiest action to take is no action at all. This study highlights that we desire a myriad of options, but we need guidance when making decisions. Without guidance, we can fall into Barry Schwartz's paradox of choice.

The placement and presentation of options influences our choices online too. In the subsequent chapters, we'll explore

---

126 Barry Schwartz, "The Paradox of Choice: Why More is Less."
127 Sheena S. Iyengar and Mark R. Lepper, "When choice is demotivating: Can one desire too much of a good thing?" 995.

how the presentation and framing of information impacts our choices. Whether it's the tweaking of a word or sentence, presenting information as a loss or gain, or taking the path of least resistance, powerful forces at play shape the path we follow. Insights into these hidden nudges can open a new world of how you think about guiding your users and helping them take the optimal path.

CHAPTER 13:

IT'S NOT WHAT YOU SAY, IT'S HOW YOU SAY IT

It's 2030, and you are the President of the United States. After a long, drawn-out election, you are sitting in the Oval Office, basking in the glory of your most recent win. It was a hard-fought campaign, but you managed to secure just enough electoral votes to put you in the White House. Your mom was right; one day, you would be President. As you sit in your office with your feet on the desk, you are interrupted.

Your Chief of Staff, Eric London, barges into the room and places a folder on your desk labeled "confidential." You reach down and open it up, only to learn there is an outbreak of a rare disease, and six hundred people have been infected in the US. The good news is that doctors have two potential solutions, but there will be consequences to either solution. Within the next day, you must pick one of the options. You cannot select both.

As the President of the United States, the decision of which program to proceed with rests in your hands. Your advisor asks you to weigh the pros and cons of each option and choose wisely. Regardless of the option selected, it will have long-lasting effects on people's lives.

You are told that if the doctors implement Program A, two hundred people will be saved. If the doctors implement Program B, there is a one-third probability that six hundred people will be saved and a two-thirds probability that no one will be saved.

You select Program A. You rationalize that it's a better bet to go with the certain option of saving two hundred people rather than rolling the dice and potentially saving no one with option B.

Four years later, the US is again struck with this disease. Once again, you're sitting in your Oval Office, minding your own business, and your Chief of Staff barges in and places a folder on the desk. You reach down, open it up to learn that there is an outbreak of this rare disease again. It's identical to the disease from four years ago. Six hundred people in the US have contracted it. Your Chief of Staff presents two potential solutions to you.

You can select Program A and four hundred people will die or select Program B where there is a one-third probability that nobody will die and a two-thirds probability that six hundred people will die.

You select Program B. You forego Program A, rationalizing that you couldn't live with yourself knowing that you chose an option that was the certain cause of four hundred deaths.

You pat yourself on the back for making the right decision and go on your way. As you lie in bed later that night, replaying both decisions in your head, a stark realization hits you. You chose Program A the first time and Program B the second time, but you come to realize that both decisions were identical, just worded differently.

In the first scenario, your Chief of Staff presented the information with a positive frame—two hundred people will be saved. In the second option, the information was presented with a negative frame—four hundred people will die. The two decisions were the same, but one is framed as a gain, and the other is framed as a loss.

In the first scenario, there is a one-third probability that six hundred people will be saved and a two-thirds probability that no one will be saved. In the second scenario, there is a one-third probability that nobody will die, and a two-thirds probability that six hundred people will die. The same information framed differently reverses our preferences.

The above hypothetical was an actual experiment run by Amos Tversky and Daniel Kahneman in 1981. It demonstrated a systematic reversal of preferences when the same information is presented in two different ways. In their research, 72 percent of the participants chose Program A when presented with the first scenario, but in the second scenario, only 22 percent selected Program A.[128,129]

Words matter, and the way information presents itself to us influences the decisions we make. We prefer a jar of ice cream that is "80 percent fat-free," but few of us would prefer ice cream that contains "20 percent fat," even though both jars contain the same amount of fat."[130]

---

128 Amos Tversky and Daniel Kahneman. "The framing of decisions and the psychology of choice." 453-458.
129 "Boundless Business: Decision Making."
130 "Why option presentation changes our decision making."

Often, when we build digital products, we forget about the significance of phrasing. We focus so much on features and design that copy falls into the background. We assume large problems warrant large, sophisticated solutions—a design overhaul, a rewrite of code, or a reimagined onboarding experience. Yet, sometimes small changes, such as a tweak of a phrase, have large effects. A company called Opower came to learn this lesson.

In 2007, Opower was founded with a simple goal: "What if we could make a better utility bill?" Throughout the company's lifespan, it raised $65 million to build a business model around energy efficiency and utility customer engagement, which took them through an IPO in 2014, and then acquisition by Oracle.[131]

Opower partners with utility companies to provide them with a platform that blends behavioral science and data analytics to engage their customers through energy reports. They help utility companies help their customers become smarter about how they use and consume energy.[132]

Julie O'Brien, who is currently the director of Behavior Change at WW, spent her early days as part of the Opower team. After earning her PhD in social psychology, she joined Opower and was a critical component in building out the company's behavioral research function. She introduced a new way of thinking, which revolutionized the way Opower went about marketing, communications and product development.

---

131 Davide Savenije, "What made Opower so successful?"
132 Ibid.

During her time at Opower, Julie and her team were working with a client based out of the United Kingdom to rethink their customer acquisition strategy. All home energy companies provide more or less the same product—energy is energy. The assumption is that when customers search for a provider, they seek out the lowest cost option. Historically, her client competed on price to win customers, but this competition sets off a chain reaction. Each company undercuts one another until they reach a point where they cannot lower prices anymore. The question Julie asked was: "How else could Opower's client compete for customers?" Julie was on a mission to decode the WHY.

Opower's client marketed toward a subset of potential customers who had just moved into a new house. The client was struggling to figure out how to convince customers to switch to their service. The client's strategy was to convince new homeowners to switch to their cheaper option. They ran numerous focus groups and interviews to collect SAY data, from which they learned that the reasons their customer made the switch was due to price.

"Of course, price does matter, but this is only part of the equation. However, since people kept mentioning price, all the solutions the team was coming up with revolved around the price: offer better deals, promote that you are the lowest cost provider, show how you compare to other energy providers," Julie commented.

"If you go through this process, though, you learn that the prices between various providers are so similar that the difference over a year is approximately $20. It's a tiny amount and typically not enough of a financial motivator to go through all of the annoying paperwork to switch energy companies for such limited savings," said Julie.

Julie and her team threw all their assumptions about what was driving behavior out the window. She asked the team, "Let's assume our standard assumption is completely wrong. What else could it be? What else could be driving switching behavior?" Julie came up with her hypothesis, one that wasn't readily apparent but rooted in research on self-regulation. Julie believed two psychological traits might be driving switching behavior.

Developed by E. Tory Higgins and Arie Kruglanski, Regulatory Mode Theory studies the development of goal-pursuit as well as motivation. The theory lays out two main approaches from a social cognition perspective regarding the pursuit of goals: one is assessment, and the other is locomotion.[133]

Scoring high on assessment means you evaluate your options before making a decision. You're the type of person who crosses all their T's and dots all the I's before making a decision—thoroughly conducting research prior to moving forward.

Julie went on to say, "You could hypothesize that people who are high on assessment are the ones who might be inclined to switch because they're willing to do all of the research and look into all of their options to make sure they're getting the best option."

Scoring high on locomotion means you need to always be doing something. You are always in motion and progressing toward something; getting things done is appealing for you.

Julie added, "You could also hypothesize that people who are willing to switch their energy provider and go through

---

133 Tory E. Higgins, Arie W. Kruglanski, and Antonio Pierro, "Regulatory mode: Locomotion and assessment as distinct orientations." 293-344.

all the paperwork and the hassle of doing it are high on locomotion. They just enjoy getting things done."

Julie created and ran a survey with a list of people who were moving their homes in the UK. She measured how the individuals scored on locomotion and assessment by asking questions that would help identify respondents into one of the two modes. Aside from collecting other demographic information, she asked questions related to price sensitivity, energy efficiency, and all the more intuitive reasons a customer would switch.

She found the results quite interesting—price sensitivity did not predict switching intentions. Instead, she found high locomotion scores and concern for saving energy were the two primary predictors of switching intention.

Armed with knowledge, Julie worked with a designer to create two email marketing campaigns. The first one focused on energy efficiency, touting that switching service providers would help the customer save energy. The second email focused on the idea of locomotion, telling the customer there is something to be done and the thing to do was to switch energy providers.

Julie tested her emails against price-centered emails, and her findings performed 3.5 times better than the price-framed emails. When users aren't converting, it can be easy to optimize the user experience to solve the issue. As evident by Julie's findings, sometimes the phrasing of an option can be the hidden secret that solves the problem.

An estate attorney living in Austin, Texas, Brantley was in search of a challenge. Spending his days writing wills for clients and working with startups, he found himself drawn to the startup scene and decided to attend a Startup Weekend event.

Startup Weekend runs fifty-four-hour weekend workshops to help founders turn ideas into reality. As Brantley walked into the workshop, he noticed everyone was a developer and spoke a different language. He decided to head for the door, figuring this wasn't his place. When he was just steps away from the exit, a guy grabbed him by the arm.

"Where are you going? You have to pitch!"

"I don't have a pitch," said Brantley.

"Yes, you do. Let me ask, what do you do in your day job that doesn't add a lot of value?" this guy asked.

"I create wills for my clients," replied Brantley.

"Perfect! That's your pitch! You give away estate planning on the internet!" the guy said.

Brantley ended up participating, pitched to eighteen teams and seven CEOs in Austin, and won Startup Weekend. On that weekend Brantley became the founder and CEO of Giving Docs. Today, Giving Docs does just that—provides estate planning online. Giving Docs focuses on helping people leave a legacy by easily assigning a portion of their will to a nonprofit of their choice.

Brantley saw the systems to help people leave their legacy to a nonprofit were antiquated and broken.

"At least 50 percent of giving bequests are not known to the organization before the individual donor passed away," Brantley added. With giving by bequest at $39.71 billion in 2018, this is a substantial amount of money for nonprofits.

While they advertised to older, wealthy individuals, nonprofits were ignoring the younger, middle-class people, a significant opportunity. The process for leaving a will was outdated and difficult to complete.

Brantley was on a mission to fix this.

After the launch of Giving Docs, Brantley saw significant initial engagement, but many users failed to complete the will executing process. The website had decent traffic, a sign of interest, but users failed to complete the entire registration process. Perplexed, Brantley and his team tweaked the registration process in hopes they could fix this problem.

"We saw early on that one of the biggest drop-off points in our funnel was when we asked people to name their executor in their will," said Brantley.

While digging into the analytics, Brantley noticed that users were leaving the site when asked to name an executor for their will. His team decided to re-architect the entire process, moving the executor step from the end to the beginning of the funnel, but results did not improve. He tried moving this step to other places in the funnel, but still nothing seemed to be working.

Perhaps the registration process wasn't broken. Perhaps there was a clue hidden in the way questions were worded. Brantley learned of a concept called mortality salience, which refers to a person's inability or unwillingness to think about dying.

"If I look at you and I tell you right now that you are going to die one day, your initial reaction is to run from that conversation and not want to talk about it," said Brantley. This question causes a chemical reaction in your brain and forces you out of the conversation. No one wants to think about their own mortality.

"If you think about it, that is the moment people imagine themselves dead. This is the moment they start thinking about their wife, or their dad, or a best friend going through their personal stuff. It's a very jarring thought, and you're asking the user to picture that," said Brantley.

Brantley then went on to add, "However, if you can get past that, you can start to think about the things that matter, what it means to you and your family, and what type of legacy you can leave behind."

Brantley had a hunch. Users were being held up by the wording of the executor question. He left the sign-up process as it was but replaced the word "executor" with words that didn't remind people of their eventual death.

With a simple tweak of wording, changing the term "executor" to "person" or "representative," the strategy worked. It didn't matter where in the funnel the question was placed, by framing the question correctly, people converted. This small change made a significant impact, and conversion rates started to climb.

Giving Docs extended this core concept to their entire business. They stopped using the term "will" altogether. Instead, they frame their offering as estate planning and avoid death messaging in their brand entirely. All of their marketing and messaging reminds people that Giving Docs is about giving, rather than dying.

"That's why we're Giving Docs. We're about giving. We're not about death."

It's easy to assume big problems need big solutions. The larger the challenge, the bigger the solution, yet a small change can have a profound impact. While design and the UX is important, don't overlook the phrasing of questions and directions in your application.

CHAPTER 14:

SOMETHING TO LOSE

As a young kid, toy trains fascinated me. Building a miniature version of a real-life world within the comforts of my bedroom amazed me. I was the creator of this pretend place lined with houses, train stops, trees, people, and forests. I'd spend hours on end in my bedroom creating, adjusting, and building that train set. I'd continuously adjust the tracks, tweaking the layout, how the trees lined the railroad, and the routes the trains took.

I remember it clearly. My source for supplies was a store called Lad's Hobby Shop, located a few miles from my childhood home. Illustrated images of toy cars, trains, and planes decorated Lad's Hobby Shop. Walking into the mall, you could see the toy store shining through an opening above the food court. I'd ask my parents to drag me there to buy a new toy train or a set of tracks so I could continue to build my train empire.

Other than my bed and a few pieces of furniture neatly tucked against the wall, my bedroom floor was empty, ready to be used as the foundation of an epic train scene. The tracks didn't lay nicely on the carpeted floors, so I purchased a large piece of wood to nail them in place. My set started small, but over time, my creation grew. Day by day, week by week, month by month, year by year, I slowly but surely acquired more tracks, bridges, turns, and train cars to build the mecca of all toy sets.

The more I built, the more pride and ownership I felt over what I had created. Each time I'd open the door to my room, the lively scene of trains roaming around the tracks would give me a sense of pride. Although I had no intention to ever sell my empire, I was certain that if the time did come, my creation would be worth quite a bit.

To a potential buyer, the fair market value of what I had built would have probably been the total cost of the materials used. But to me, the set was worth much more. After all, I had created it; it came from my mind, and even though I wasn't an expert, to me, what I had built was miraculous.

Gains and losses, how do we value them and how do we perceive them? In 1979, Daniel Kahneman and Amos Tversky developed prospect theory, a founding theory of behavioral economics that seeks to understand how we assess losses and gains.[134]

We don't view gains and losses in the same way. Instead, losses psychologically feel twice as great as an equal gain. Imagine walking down the street and stumbling across a $20 bill, and then later that day, you lose the $20 bill. A $20 loss is felt psychologically as a $40 loss; it stings twice as much. Our loss aversion impacts our decision-making in interesting ways.

---

134 Amos Tversky and Daniel Kahneman, "Prospect theory: An analysis of decision under risk." 263-291.

According to classical economics and traditional microeconomic theory, only prospective (future) costs are relevant to a rational decision, but we fall prey to the sunk cost fallacy. We take incurred costs into account—costs that are in the past and cannot be recovered.[135] We place a greater value on objects that we had a hand in making regardless of their economic value to others.

A study by Michael I. Norton, Daniel Mochon, and Dan Ariely, "The IKEA Effect: When Labor Leads to Love," notes this phenomenon.[136] In a series of studies, participants assembled IKEA boxes, folded origami, and built sets of Legos. They demonstrate and investigate the boundary conditions for what they termed the "IKEA effect," which describes the increase in the valuation of self-made products.

While the participants weren't experts, they saw their creation as ones created by experts. The saying "Labor of Love" holds true; they valued their creations more than others would, not because these creations were objectively better, but simply because they had built them. Could the same concept help users follow through on goals to become healthier? If we give users more ownership of their plan of action, will more of them follow through?

The US is experiencing an obesity problem. From 2017 to 2018, 42.4 percent of Americans were considered obese. Obesity contributes to an increase in coronary artery disease, type

---

135 James Chen, "Sunk Cost Dilemma."
136 Michael I. Norton, Daniel Mochon, and Dan Ariely, "The IKEA effect: When labor leads to love." 453-460.

2 diabetes, and strokes. Aside from health concerns, it also results in a significant economic impact with an obese person incurring an average of $1,429 more in medical expenses over a year.[137]

Losing weight is hard and keeping it off is even harder. Overweight individuals hold good intentions. They want to exercise more, eat healthier, and shed the extra pounds, but there is a myriad of reasons why 95 percent of diets fail. A new app, Noom, is here to change that.

Artem Petakov, founder of Noom, started programming when he was nine years old. During his time majoring in computer science at Princeton, he found himself drawn to developmental psychology books. After falling in love with the psychology of decision-making, he took classes with Daniel Kahneman. At its core, Noom combines two of Artem's passions: technology and psychological science.

Artem and his cofounder, Saeju, use several of technology's most advanced tactics to help users live healthier lives by combining the power of AI, mobile tech, and an understanding of what drives behavior to help users stick around and become healthier versions of themselves. The company gives users access to over one thousand personal coaches to help them stay on track and supplements the coaches with a personalized weight loss plan that users have access to 24/7.

Losing weight is hard for a myriad of reasons. One, you're asking a user to commit to taking action today for potential, uncertain benefits in the distant future. The psychological headwinds are working against us, and Noom knows this. To ensure Noom users will stick with their weight loss plan,

---

137 CDC, "Adult Obesity Facts."

the company forces them to invest in their own success during the signup process.

I decided to find out for myself.

I navigate to the website and start the registration process. Rather than asking me for my name and email address as the first step, Noom asks me to input my ideal weight and proceeds to collect various pieces of demographic information such as my height, gender, and age.

As I move through a few questions, the process feels arduous. I wonder how long this process is going to take and contemplate calling it quits. Just as I get to the point where I am about to exit the process, a message pops up that reminds me of my goal and nudges me to continue: "Noom creates long-term results through habit and behavior change, not restrictive dieting." I keep going.

At this point in the process, Noom asks me a few questions related to my weight loss goals. I tell the app that I am in my thirties, and my ideal weight is 175 lbs. After entering this information, I see a message:

> "Men in their 30s who want to reach an ideal weight between 165 lbs. and 185 lbs. need a slightly different strategy depending on their current lifestyle. Which best describes you?"
> My diet and activity need a lot of work
> I have some healthy habits
> I mostly eat well and stay active

Noom knows I am in my thirties. Is it chance Noom is referencing men in their thirties? I was curious. Based on my information, is Noom dynamically changing the message? I decided to find out.

I navigate back and change my answers. This time, I input that I am a forty-year-old female with an ideal weight of 125 lbs. I hit "next," and sure enough, the message now reads:

> *"Women in their 40s who want to reach an ideal weight between 115 lbs. and 135 lbs. need a slightly different strategy depending on their current lifestyle. Which best describes you?"*
> *My diet and activity need a lot of work*
> *I have some healthy habits*
> *I mostly eat well and stay active*

I tested this a few more times by changing several of my answers, and it confirmed my hypothesis: Noom is dynamically changing the experience based on my previous answers.

When I see "Men in their 30s…" I cannot help but think, "Wow, that's me!" I am under the impression that Noom understands my situation.

I am then presented with questions about my lifestyle, such as:

What is your main reason for wanting to lose weight? (Please choose what is most important.)

Which of the below best describes your current priorities?

Notice the consultative approach Noom takes with their registration process. I feel as if I am sitting in a room talking to another person who wants to get to know me and *why* I am on this journey.

Noom is personalizing my experience and leveraging the endowment effect, allowing me to play a role in building *my* plan, giving me the sense that this plan is created just for me. With ownership over my plan, I am likely to invest back into the program since I built it.

Remember, at this point, I had changed my registration information and identified myself as a female. After I complete the next two questions, a testimonial from a happy customer in her mid-thirties to forties appears.

"Noom fits into my lifestyle perfectly. I can turn to this app day or night and they're there for me."

~ *Jennifer.*

Providing social proof is a common technique, but I am curious. Are the testimonials dynamic too? After all, the information I am seeing is changing based on my answers.

Once again, I navigate back and change my gender to male. Sure enough, I arrive at the testimonial section and the gender of the testimonial changes too. A male who looks to be in his mid-thirties greets me.

> *"Noom changes the way I think about portion control. It changed my relationship with food."*
>
> ~ Mike

Noom is dynamically changing the gender of the person giving the testimonial based on my gender. If I elect that I am female, they show a female testimonial. If I select that I am male, they show a male testimonial. Through this similarity, Noom is gaining my trust.

As alluded to in an earlier chapter, we trust people who are similar to us in terms of demographic information. We trust people who look and act like us. The more someone is like us, the more likely we are to trust their opinion.[138] Mike

---

138 Harry T. Reis, "Similarity-attraction effect." 875-876.

isn't too different than me and without good reason, I believe him. Noom has helped him, so Noom can help me.

I arrive at the final step of the onboarding form, and the page reads, *"We've helped 32,905 men in their 30s successfully reach their target weight."* Once again they reinforce that Noom helps other men just like me hit their target weight.

Over the course of thirty seconds, a loading bar fills up and reads:

Connecting to database ...
Preparing Results ...

Noom asks me to input my email address to see my plan results.

Most applications prompt you to enter in your email address as the first step of the sign-up process. Noom strategically places this after I invest considerable time and effort into building my plan. I now have much more to lose by exiting the website. I've spent significant time and energy filling out their questions, and if I don't enter my email address, all of that will go to waste.

Noom presents me with a button to "See My Result" in exchange for entering my email address.

I enter my email address and click: "See My Result." After a few seconds, a new page loads.

"Based on your answers, you'll be ... 172 lbs. by June 4th."

Noom has set a goal for me to reach, one that is measurable, attainable, and built by me. This tactic reinforces that the Noom is building the plan for me.

Finally, a button reads, "Claim my plan." The button does not say "view plan" or "open plan," it reads "claim plan." This phrasing conveys that this "plan" exists, and it's waiting for me to make it mine. After all, I don't want to leave something behind that has been created just for me.

I click "claim my plan," and I assume the process is complete, but something interesting happens. I am only halfway there.

"Halfway there! Now let's customize your plan. Please take your time when answering. Each response is used to create your personalized program."

Noom's onboarding process is long. Imagine if Noom had presented me with a fifty-question form at the beginning of the process. I would have exited immediately. Noom's strategic approach of breaking up the process into smaller segments while ensuring I am investing into the process along my journey keeps my attention.

Noom continues to ask me questions:

Have any life events led to weight gain in the last few years?
How long has it been since you were at your ideal weight?
Have you attempted any of the following in the past to help lose weight?
Has your weight ever affected your ability to socialize or engage with friends and family?
What area do you want to focus on first in your plan?

Notice again the consultative tone of these questions. These questions aren't necessary for Noom to create my personalized program; they are structured in a way to set me up for success. Noom *understands me* and is here to help me on my journey, and the phrasing of their onboarding questions conveys this.

As I answer the questions, I feel as if I am sitting in a room with a health coach. He is letting me know that even though I may have failed at this before, it's okay. The reason is because I haven't found the right strategy, not because I am a failure, and he is here with me along my journey.

The program then asks me if I relate to any of the following statements:

> *"I know what I should be doing to lose weight, but I need a way to do it that fits into MY life."*
> *"I need some outside motivation. When I am feeling overwhelmed, it can be easy to give up."*
> *"I have been thinking about weight loss for a while, but life is so busy I find myself putting convenience first."*

The answer to all of these questions is yes. Noom is taking the words right of my mouth. Rather than berating me for failing at a plan before, Noom's wording makes me think, "Finally! Someone understands!"

Noom asks me questions about my marital status, alcoholic beverages, and how busy I am on an average day. Just at the point where the questions are feeling burdensome and I contemplate exiting, Noom leverages the authority bias by showing me that reputable institutions endorse Noom.

> *"Columbia University reports that 73 percent of dieters experience at least one weight cycling episode."*
> *"The Mayo Clinic reports more 'Yo-Yo' cycles increase diabetes risk and amounts of belly fat."*

Noom asks me to create an account. After I click this, Noom tells me it's creating my customized plan and building three main sections of my plan. A progress bar can be seen filling up from 0 percent to 100 percent for each of the following:

Demographic Profile
Habits and Behaviors
Activity and Nutrition

These results are instantaneously calculated, but booking sites such as Hotels.com or Kayak use this tactic to give the impression that the site is working hard behind the scenes to create a plan that is custom for me.[139] If Noom is doing work behind the scenes to create my plan, it must be valuable. Built explicitly for me, it can't be cookie-cutter.

The final step asks me to claim my plan. At this point in the process, I am fully invested not only in the plan, but also the company itself. Not only have I spent fifteen minutes building my plan, but I have disclosed personal information about my fitness journey. I've revealed to this company where I have failed, where I have succeeded, and what success looks like for me. I am invested in the outcome because I helped build it.

Noom's registration process was long and arduous, requiring a significant time investment. Contrary to best practices that recommend a registration processes that is as short as possible, Noom has done the opposite with upward of twenty questions that can take fifteen minutes to complete.

---

139 Ryan W. Buell and Michael I. Norton, "Think Customers Hate Waiting? Not So Fast...."

Why would Noom create a registration process that is so cumbersome? Wouldn't this decrease the likelihood a user would complete the process? Common sense would say yes, but behavioral science says otherwise. The more of a hand we have in creating something, the less likely we are to part with it. While some may drop out of the process early, those who complete it are more likely to stick with their plans. You substitute quality for quantity.

Not only does this increase the likelihood I will try the Noom program, but it sets me up for long-term success. This weight loss plan was not given to me by Noom. Instead, it was created by me with the help of the Noom team.

How effective is their approach? In 2016, researchers conducted a study to find out. They analyzed data from 35,921 users who recorded their diet at least twice per month over six months. The approach seemed to be working, 77.9 percent reported a reduction in body weight, and users who monitored their weight and dietary habits experienced more consistent weight loss.[140,141]

The success Noom has achieved to date goes beyond just their technical capabilities. The blend of behavioral science and AI has enabled Noom to build an app that is helping solve a major health crisis in the US, and they are just getting started.

"We are starting with weight loss and diabetes prevention and expanding to other conditions. In the US, 72 percent of the population is either overweight or obese, which is often the gateway into comorbidities. 69.8 percent of Noom users reported they were at risk for one or more other serious health conditions (diabetes, hypertension, etc.)," said Artem.

---

140 Jessica Caporuscio, "Everything you need to know about the Noom diet."
141 Sang Ouk Chin, et al, "Successful weight reduction and maintenance by using a smartphone application in those with overweight and obesity." 1-8.

Noom helps deliver diabetes prevention programs too. In 2016, the company recruited forty-three participants with pre-diabetes. After using the app, the participants had experienced weight loss by week sixteen and week twenty-four. After the study, thirty-six participants completed the program, and of those, 64 percent lost more than 5 percent of their total body weight.[142,143]

Giving your users the ability to invest in their future gives them more ownership over it. While creating an extensive onboarding process may run contrary to best practices, in some instances this long initial up-front investment can pay dividends for you and your users in the long term.

---

142 Jessica Caporuscio, "Everything you need to know about the Noom diet."
143 Andreas Michaelides, et al, "Weight loss efficacy of a novel mobile Diabetes Prevention Program delivery platform with human coaching."

CHAPTER 15:

THE POWER OF PEANUTS AND DEFAULTS

Every day, more than 130 people in the United States die from overdosing on opioids. The misuse and addiction to this deadly medication has become a severe national crisis.[144] One contributing factor is the over-prescription of pills. Doctors are giving patients more pills then they need, and it's contributing to addiction and overdoses.

The Center for Disease Control (CDC) provides instructions on how opioids should be prescribed and taken.[145] Provided with correct guidance, doctors should follow instructions. After all, doctors don't want people to get addicted; they're not intentionally overprescribing pills to patients. Nonetheless, equipped with accurate information, doctors were still overprescribing pills.

At one hospital, upward of 40 percent of doctors were overprescribing pills to their patients. While this issue is vast

---

144 "Opioid Overdose Crisis."
145 Kristen Berman, "How behavioral scientists build products."

and complex and no single solution can solve it, behavioral science may hold a clue into what is going on.[146]

To define what was driving the problem, researchers effectively conducted a behavioral diagnosis, mapping out the entire journey a doctor went through while writing a prescription. Researchers identified points within the process that could be leading to overprescribing pills.

After much research, it seemed they had come across their needle in the haystack. The doctors were following precisely what the system was telling them to do.

The default number shown in the medical software was thirty. There was no rhyme or reason as to why thirty was the default as opposed to ten, or twenty, or five. Researchers hypothesized that these doctors took the default amount of thirty to mean that thirty was the expected number of pills to give.

They decided to test their assumption by changing the default number in the system from thirty pills to twelve pills. When they did, the number of doctors prescribing thirty pills dropped from 40 percent to 13 percent, a difference of 27 percent. A simple tweak of a number had a significant impact.

"When you change that default or norm, rationally, nothing should happen. A doctor is an expert; they've done this for a while. There is no reason the person designing the form field should have any influence on the number of pills the expert doctor prescribes. And yet, even for experts, a seemingly small change in the environment changed their behavior," said Kristen Berman, cofounder of Irrational Labs.[147]

---

146 Alexander S. Chiu, et al, "Association of lowering default pill counts in electronic medical record systems with postoperative opioid prescribing." 1012-1019.
147 Kristen Berman, "How behavioral scientists build products."

Intentional or not, setting thirty as the default implied a norm. Doctors may have thought this number *was* the recommended number. Perhaps the doctors assumed the creators of the software conducted research and displayed the number thirty for a reason. Doctors had no reason to believe this number was selected with intention, yet they may have assumed, as we all do, that defaults are provided with good reason. Someone who knows *better* than I do must have recommended this option.

"If you were to ask doctors what would help them from overprescribing, they would never tell you that the software was influencing their decision-making, even though it was," Kristen added. Without knowledge of behavioral science, researchers wouldn't have looked for this hidden clue.

We resist change. When presented with a choice in which Option A adheres to the current situation and Option B is to change, we have a disproportionate preference for Option A. We prefer the default, the way things are—if a particular choice is defaulted, it automatically becomes our status quo, and our cognitive interpretation of it shifts. It is now the recommended option, and any deviation from it presents a risk. This bias is one of the seminal findings illustrating the importance of how choices are presented, merely manipulating the default option can dramatically shift preferences.[148]

The default bias affects all of us, often referred to as the status quo bias. We leave things as they are. Previous findings provide ample evidence in both retirement program

---

148 Cass R. Sunstein, "With Clean-Energy Default Rules, It's Easy Being Green."

and health insurance plan selection indicating that individuals are very unlikely to opt-out as a result of inertia caused by status quo bias, or a preference for the current state of affairs.[149]

Defaults are powerful, and the concept extends beyond just changing a number on a screen. Imagine being in a job that no longer fulfilled your needs.

Every day, you wake up dreading walking into the office; your pay is below what you deserve to be making, and the work doesn't challenge you. You want to leave the job, but the choice to go is a difficult one. Leaving brings with it a myriad of unknowns about what the future holds and inherent risks, so year after year, you remain at your job. You feel that since you didn't make a decision, life has continued on its predestined course.

Even though your decision to stay at your job is still a decision, this is not how you see it. You see, the decision *not* to make a decision is life continuing on its predestined path. Yet, if you decide to leave and end up regretting the choice, you made an active decision that impacted the outcome. This trajectory is no longer life's normal state of affairs because you intervened, and your choice led to a suboptimal outcome.

We don't want to be the reason we made the wrong decision. We divert to the path of least resistance, leaving things the way they are even if it's not in our best interest. There is comfort in leaving things the way they are, letting them naturally continue along their course. We lean toward inaction because taking action means we have a hand in destiny,

---

149 . William Samuelson and Richard Zeckhauser, "Status quo bias in decision making." 7-59.

and if destiny doesn't turn out the way we intended, we can only blame ourselves.[150]

If defaults are powerful enough to change the prescription practices of doctors, where else could this be applied? Three friends pondered if a similar approach could help people give more money to charity.

Nick Fritz sat with his good friends Ari Kagan and Ivan Dimitrov on a deck, drinking a few beers and kicking around business ideas. Having previously worked at Duke University's Center for Advanced Hindsight under the direction of Dan Ariely, Nick and Ari are well-versed in helping startups scale through a behavioral-first approach.

During Nick's time at the lab he focused on the psychology of giving; striving to understand what moves people to give. Nick and Ari wondered how their learnings from their time at Duke could help increase giving amounts.

Acorns, an easy to use finance app, was growing exponentially, and Nick and Ari pondered why something similar did not exist in the charity space. The beauty of these products is that they make investing simple and easy. These products are more than a sleek design. They counter the psychological mechanisms at play preventing us from being more responsible with our money.

Saving is hard. You're asking users to perform an action today where the potential payouts are far in the distant future. Acorns, built from the ground up leveraging behavioral science, sees success through its use of defaults and the peanuts

---

150 Sümeyra Gazel, "The Regret Aversion as an Investor Bias." 419-424.

effect. The brilliance of the app is in its design of defaults and framing savings contributions as small amounts, where frequent tiny deposits can have a significant impact as they accumulate over time.

Acorns helps people invest in the future by rounding up spare change. For example, if you spend $3.87, Acorns will round it up to the nearest dollar amount and invest the difference into several investment vehicles. When spending $3.87, incurring an additional loss of thirteen cents feels inconsequential, especially in the context of paying $3.87. This effect, the peanuts effect, is when we fail to consider the consequences of small losses.[151] In this case, it is a good thing.

The peanuts effect is part of the reason slot machines steal all of our money. Fifty cents here, a dollar here, fifty more cents here feels like little money, but turn around after playing the machine for two hours, and you've spent upward of two hundred dollars. We are insensitive to small numbers, and this effect is part of the brilliance of Acorns.

To encourage users to opt into a recurring savings plan, Acorns experiments with various ways to frame the savings amounts. In a recent study, Noah, the CEO of Acorns wondered if breaking down the investments into smaller increments increased user uptake.

"You can add a recurring investment by the day, week, or month," notes Noah.

One of the first experiments looked at whether customers would rather save $5 per day, $35 per week, or $150 monthly. The sum is roughly the same, yet only 7 percent of people

---

[151] Kazumi Shimizu and Daisuke Udagawa, "Is human life worth peanuts? Risk attitude changes in accordance with varying stakes."

opted for the monthly option of $150, while 30 percent agreed to save $5 a day.

Saving $150 per month is painful because you imagine saving $150 at once. Saving $5 per day for a month, however, is doable. You imagine parting with $5 today and you fail to take into account the daily $5 deposits in the future.

The decision to save is easier when framed in a way that spreads the potential losses into smaller increments over time.[152] Their approach seems to be working. The company had two million investment accounts under management as of January 28, 2019.

Could learnings from Acorns translate to helping people give? The team at Momentum thinks so.

The surface-level problem seemed glaringly obvious to Nick and his team—donating online was difficult. In the SAY data, donors explained that they donate less than they intend to because the process of giving is unnecessarily difficult. With this in mind, the solution seemed simple, even glaringly evident to Nick. Make it as seamless as possible to complete a donation online.

"Part of the challenge of helping people give more was just poor design on nonprofits' websites, it is much harder to donate than it is to complete a purchase on Amazon," noted Nick.

Although multiple products make online giving easy, online donation rates are extremely low. As of 2018, online donations only made up 8.5 percent of total nonprofit fundraising.[153] Numerous websites allow donors to donate and manage their giving similar to how one would manage a

---

152 Ryan W. Neal, "Shlomo Benartzi to chair Acorns behavioral economics committee."
153 Steve MacLaughlin, Chuck Longfield, and Angele Vellake, "Charitable Giving Report: How Nonprofit Fundraising Performed in 2018."

stock portfolio. Gain access to an online portal, quickly search for a nonprofit and make a donation, but none of these platforms have seen success.

If the problem was so glaringly obvious, why had so many other products failed to gain traction? These startups are addressing the wrong issue because they are asking the wrong question. While making it easy for donors to give online is a problem that needs fixing, this isn't where the real behavioral drivers lie.

Given Nick's background, he had a hunch there was more to the SAY data. Instead of taking the problem at face value, Nick and his team dug deep into the behavioral science literature to decode what was really going on.

The real challenge lay hidden in the intention-action gap. People want to give more but often find themselves falling short of their goals.[154]

"We have found that people want to give about two and a half times more than they currently do. Most people want to give more than they already do, but life gets in the way," said Nick.

"How do we make giving easy, not just in terms of the user experience, but in terms of removing the behavioral mechanisms that are preventing people from giving time and again?" Nick added.

Parting with money is painful, no matter how large or how small the amount, there is pain associated when we part with our hard-earned money. His team at Momentum leverages the default bias and the peanuts effect to help everyday people close their intention-action gap. Momentum's giving rules pair significant events and daily actions with automatic

---

154 Omar Parbhoo, "I Think, Therefore I Am—Generous?"

donations to any nonprofit in the country. Momentum's brilliant system allows users to set up a small recurring donation triggered by a purchase or event.

Their product leverages the default bias in several ways. First, the default way to give is recurring, not one-time. Furthermore, even when selecting rules, default options make it simple for the user to get started. If you decide to donate every time you purchase a cup of coffee, the app defaults to a $1 donation.

Can't think of a cause to donate to, check out the "popular" section, which has predetermined default rules you can opt into. For example, every-time Trump tweets, you can automatically donate $0.10 to the ACLU. Or, whenever a new major #MeToo scandal is exposed, you donate $15 to women's empowerment organizations. Or, whenever you purchase a cup of coffee, you donate $1 to helping people get access to clean water. Donate $.10 here, $.50 here, $1 here, and before you know it, in a few months, you've made a large impact. Each donation is peanuts, a dollar here, a dollar there, ten cents here, fifty cents there, but over time, these small donations add up to large amounts.

In life, we often take the path of least resistance. Our tendency to follow the status quo is subtle yet powerful, and digital experiences are no exception to this rule. As you build, ask yourself: "What is the action I want my user to complete, and how can I make it as easy as possible?"

CHAPTER 16:

DRIVEN BY EMOTION

It is 7 a.m. on a Monday. After completing a swim at my local pool, I walk over to my coffee shop a few blocks away. "Cold brew, please, light ice."

Within seconds, a coffee is placed on the counter. "Excuse me, do you have any more straws?" I ask.

"Oh, no, we got rid of our straws. They're destroying the oceans," said the barista.

I glance back at my cup and notice a new type of lid. The lid itself is still plastic, but it now has a small opening in the shape of a triangle, eliminating the need for a plastic straw.

Huh? Interesting, I thought.

Are plastic straws that big of a problem? I support reducing plastic waste in our oceans, but I was surprised to hear this had caught on. When and how did this straw ban gain momentum? I decided to do some research.

Relative to the plastic pollution in our oceans, straws account for a tiny portion. Eight million tons of plastic flow into the ocean every year, and straws comprise just 0.025 percent of that.[155,156]

---

155 Jenna R. Jambeck, et al, "Plastic waste inputs from land into the ocean." 768-771.
156 Seth Borenstein, "Science Says: Amount of straws, plastic pollution is huge."

As of the beginning of July 2018, Seattle became the largest US city to ban plastic straws, and many others in both the private and public sectors are following suit all around the world.[157] As of when this book was written, Starbucks was planning to phase out plastic straws by 2020, and McDonald's recently announced it would ban plastic straws at its UK and Ireland restaurants.[158,159] Last May, Bon Appétit Management, a food service company, announced it would phase out plastic straws.160 As of January 1, 2019, a ban on plastic straws in restaurants and other service businesses began in Washington, DC.[161]

Much to my surprise, the straw ban had been in place in DC since 2014, but everyone simply ignored it, and the government didn't enforce the ban. In 2019 the crackdown began. Why had a ban that had been in place since 2014 not taken off until 2019? It was because of one photo.

"At first, it looked like a worm," said Christine Figgener, a sea turtle expert at Texas A&M University in College Station who helped an injured reptile off the coast of Costa Rica.[162] You may have seen the image I am referring to. It is gruesome—a picture of a turtle in agonizing pain with a straw lodged in its nose. The mouth of the turtle hangs open. As a stream of blood flows down the nose of the turtle, signaling to us the pain the poor creature is in. Evident from the

---

157 "Food Service Packaging Requirements."
158 Bonnie Rochman, "Straws are out, lids are in: Starbucks announces environmental milestone."
159 Emily Beament, "McDonald's to ban plastic straws in all of its restaurants in UK and Ireland."
160 Zlati Meyer, "Big food-service outfit banning plastic straws at more than 1,000 US eateries."
161 Jacob Fenston, "Plastic Straws Now Officially Banned in DC"
162 Jane J. Lee, "How Did Sea Turtle Get a Straw Up Its Nose?"

straw's faded color, it has likely been lodged in the nose of this helpless turtle for weeks, if not months.

What about this photo kicked a straw ban into action?

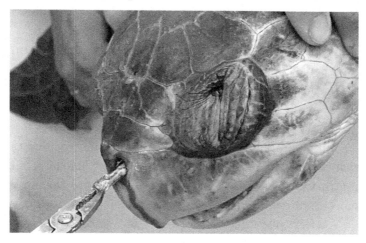

Behavioral science addresses a theory known as the Identifiable Victim Effect, which seeks to understand what moves us to offer help. We have a greater tendency to offer help when a single, "identifiable" victim is observed in a distressing situation versus a group of people.[163] The image of a single, identifiable victim, the turtle, explains part of the phenomenon of the viral straw ban.

We process information about one identifiable person, victim, or beneficiary differently than information about a group of people. Our brain processes information more quickly

---

163 Karen Jenni and George Loewenstein, "Explaining the identifiable victim effect." 235-257.

when there is one person as opposed to two, three, or more. Even for a group as small as two people, we can't process the information as quickly. When moving from two to three to four people, the intensity of this effect decreases. This group of people is more abstract and, therefore, less emotional.

When seeing individuals, we naturally group them together by specific characteristics such as age, location, background, or other demographic factors. Just as we arbitrarily group unrelated items into a set, we do this with people too. We make generalizations.[164]

With an individual, we attribute specific information to that person. Because of this, we are not only able to recall information faster, but it's also more concrete and, therefore, more emotional.

You feel empowered because you're saving that one person. However, not only the identifiable victim captivates us, but also the story behind that victim. Numbers don't connect with us in the same way stories do. Our brains are very poor at understanding and visualizing numerical data. It's difficult to visualize large quantities of anything.

"We saved twelve million turtles last year." How many is twelve million? Can you visualize twelve million in your head? When we don't value the scale of a problem in relation to its size, we fall prey to scope insensitivity.[165] The larger the problem, the more effort we should put toward solving it, but this is not the case. We don't offer aid in a way that correlates to the size and scope of the issue because we base our decisions on emotion rather than numbers.

---

164 Daniel M. Oppenheimer and Christopher Y. Olivola, eds., *The Science of Giving: Experimental Approaches to the Study of Charity.*

165 Daniel Kahneman, "Maps of Bounded Rationality: Psychology for Behavioral Economists."

Identifiable victims serve as their own reference group. If an identifiable victim dies, 100 percent of their group is dead, and the mission has failed. If a statistical victim dies, they generally represent a tiny percentage of the overall "group" in need of saving.[166] As the saying goes, "The death of a person is a tragedy, but the death of a million people is a statistic."

In the photo of this single turtle, we could see its pain. It was tangible, concrete, and helpless; it moved us emotionally in a way that numbers and statistics cannot and created a sense that we could save *that* turtle.

Think back to a powerful marketing campaign, and you'll recall that it revolved around stories. Innovative companies move you emotionally through stories to sell you a product or service. Nike is an athletic wear company, but much of its marketing revolves around stories of athletes progressing through the Hero's Journey.[167]

Driven by emotion, we make decisions based on feelings rather than facts. We think about and process the world in stories. The best sales pitches and advocacy campaigns revolve around stories. When we hear a story, we place ourselves in the shoes of the main character, understanding their journey, their hardships, their ups and downs, and their success.

---

166 Karen Jenni and George Loewenstein, "Explaining the identifiable victim effect." 235-257.
167 Kevin O'Sullivan, "The Best Writing Formula for Epic Marketing Content."

On an episode of Hidden Brain, Vera Tobin adds, "Stories are what happen to us as we make our way through the world. All the time, we're making inferences, we're trying to make sense of the world and understand what other people think, what other people know, what's going on, and what stories do is they play on these tendencies, and they exploit them to create pyrotechnic effects."[168]

Stories contain recognizable patterns, and within those patterns, we find meaning. This tendency is so innate that we find story patterns even where they don't exist. We use stories to share knowledge with others and pass lessons about our past down to our children. Stories connect us and carry on traditions, rituals, and lessons from generation to generation.

Anthropologists tell us that storytelling is central to human existence. It's common to every known culture and religion, a symbolic exchange between listener and teller.[169] It's how we learn life's greatest lessons and make sense of the world. Stories helps us make sense of the world around us, to understand what may lie ahead based on what happened in the past.

Known as neural coupling, stories activate parts of the brain that enable the listener to turn the story into their own ideas and experiences. When we hear a story, various areas of the brain are activated such as the motor cortex, sensory cortex, and frontal cortex.[170] When listening to a story, we experience similar brain activity not only to other listeners, but also to the speaker. When experiencing an

---

168 Shankar Vedantam, et al, "Tell Me A Story: What Narratives Reveal About the Mind."
169 Frank Rose, "The Art of Immersion: Why Do We Tell Stories?"
170 "Infographic: The Science of Storytelling."

emotionally charged event, the brain releases dopamine, making it easier for us to accurately remember information we're hearing.

Brady Josephson, Managing Director of NextAfter Institute, notes, "Stories and storytelling are something we are fundamentally hard-wired for." [171]

How do you create a powerful story to capture your audience?

Joseph John Campbell was an American Professor of Literature at Sarah Lawrence College who worked in comparative mythology and comparative religion. Campbell's most well-known work is his book, *The Hero with a Thousand Faces* (1949), in which he discusses his theory of the journey of the archetypal hero shared by world mythologies, termed the monomyth. The central pattern most studied by Campbell, the Hero's Journey, was first described in *The Hero with a Thousand Faces*. [172]

Campbell lays out the Hero's Journey in twelve distinct stages. I challenge you to think of a famous movie or book, and you probably can fit the plot of the story into the framework below.

- **Ordinary World**—the hero is living in a normal world.
- **Call to Adventure**—he or she gets called to some type of adventure.
- **Refusal of the Call**—the hero refuses the call and goes back to ordinary life.

---

[171] Brady Josephson, "The Science Behind Storytelling and How to Use The Pixar Framework."
[172] Joseph Campbell, *The Hero with a Thousand Faces.*

- **Meeting the Mentor**—the hero meets with a mentor; this can be an actual person or symbolic, but someone who is going to show the hero the way.
- **Crossing the Threshold**—the hero is now ready to act; the hero may go willingly or unwilling but begins his quest.
- **Tests, Allies, Enemies**—the hero faces several tests and tribulations.
- **Approach to the Inmost Cave**—unknowingly, the hero approaches his biggest challenge yet; he may begin to question his abilities. This section helps the audience understand the magnitude of the ordeal that awaits the hero and escalates the tension in anticipation of his ultimate test.
- **Ordeal**—this is where the hero has his ultimate test. It may be with an external force or inner.
- **Reward (Seizing the Sword)**—after succeeding, the hero arrives in a new state, a new person, and often with some type of material or spiritual reward.
- **The Road Back**—the hero is on the way back home with his or her newfound reward.
- **Resurrection**—the hero has his final encounter and most significant challenge, yet he encounters his most dangerous challenge and beats his final enemy.
- **Return with the Elixir**—this is where the hero returns home a new person.

Another popular story framework was put forth in Dan Pink's book, To Sell Is Human, in which he deconstructs some of Pixar's secret sauce. [173]

---

[173] Daniel H. Pink. *To Sell Is Human: The Surprising Truth about Moving Others.*

The format goes like this:

Once upon a time...
Every day...
One day...
Because of that...
Because of that...
Until finally...

In his book, Pink uses *Finding Nemo* as an example for the Pixar pitch framework:

Once upon a time, there was a widowed fish named Marlin who was extremely protective of his only son, Nemo.
Every day, Marlin warned Nemo of the ocean's dangers and implored him not to swim far away.
One day in an act of defiance, Nemo ignores his father's warnings and swims into the open water.
Because of that, he is captured by a diver and ends up as a pet in the fish tank of a dentist in Sydney.
Because of that, Marlin sets off on a journey to recover Nemo, enlisting the help of other sea creatures along the way.
Until finally, Marlin and Nemo find each other, reunite, and learn that love depends on trust.

In Robert Sapolsky's book, *Behave,* he notes that three layers divide our brain. The first layer of the brain is the most ancient part of the brain and regulates functions that we can't turn off even if we want to: heartbeat, breathing, etc. The second part is the emotional part. When we're happy, sad, angry, or nervous, we can somewhat override this part of the brain, but these reactions are instinctual.

The third layer is for memory storage, cognition, philosophy, etc. The third layer is the part of the brain where complex thinking happens, where you do complex calculations or create new strategies for the latest project you're working on.[174]

To move people emotionally, tap into layer two and convey the emotional experience to your audience. How do we tap into layer two of the brain, the emotional side, to move people to action?

We are visual machines. The brain can identify images seen for as little as thirteen milliseconds.[175] In the absence of verbal or written communication, we can understand complex emotional and mental states. We're good at identifying objects, but we're even better at identifying faces.

According to the Association for Psychological Science, there are at least 3.7 x 1016 different expression combinations, which is about the same probabilistic space as the same person winning two Powerball jackpots.[176] Within milliseconds, our brains identify a person's expression and make a connection between what that person is showing and what they may be feeling. Neuroscientists still don't know exactly how we perceive and understand each other's emotions, but they have some insight. This ability is something we're born with. Research proves that babies can recognize the shape of a face before they are born.[177]

How do we come to understand emotions? Where is the information about one's emotional state derived? Recall the last striking piece of imagery you saw; did you

---

174 Ibid.
175 Anne Trafton, "In the blink of an eye."
176 "We Read Emotions Based on How the Eye Sees."
177 Hannah Nichols, "Babies recognize face-like patterns before birth."

notice the person's eyes? We are moved emotionally when we can see an individual's eyes. We garner 85 percent of the information about a person's emotional state through their eyes. William Shakespeare once said, "The eyes are a window into the soul," and while he may not have understood the neuroscience behind his phrase, the accuracy of it holds.[178,179]

The photo above illustrates this. Simply by looking at this child's eyes you understand how she feels safe, secure and content in what looks to be her father's arms. Stories connect with us in ways facts cannot, a lesson that a nonprofit called charity:water understands quite well. How to integrate stories was a lesson Jason Kermadis learned when he came on board as their Chief Product Officer.

---

178 "Eye Reading (Body Language)."
179 David Ludden, "Your Eyes Really Are the Window to the Soul."

Jason started his career in 1996. He was working with high growth startups in Silicon Valley, where the motto is "move fast and break stuff," and the culture is to test often and iterate quickly. In this world, companies must always be pushing the envelope and developing the next best thing or risk being put out of business by a competitor.

In 2000, he moved to NYC to help start Active Buddy, which was the first chatbot to use natural language processing. After a few other stints and attending Stern Business School in New York, he got back into the interactive space with Everyday Health, working on their product for medical professionals. He then joined Audible, a company that enables users to listen to audiobooks. Little did he know, the lessons he learned from his time at these high-growth startups would translate to helping solve the water crisis.

Charity:water is a nonprofit organization bringing clean, safe drinking water to people in developing countries.[180] 100 percent of public donations go to water projects. I walk into their New York City office, and the walls lined with eight-foot-tall photos of men, women, and children holding the iconic yellow water jug—a symbol of charity:water. The images are so large I feel as if I am instantly transported into their world, standing side by side with the beneficiaries of clean water. Their smiles are infectious. I can instantly feel the good charity:water is doing.

For any organization, nonprofit or for-profit, a reliable stream of revenue is critical for growth. Knowing they have guaranteed funds coming in enables them to plan for the

---

180 "Our Mission." Charity: Water.

future. In an age where consumer purchasing behaviors are changing, where paying for a product or service on a subscription basis is becoming the norm, this presents a massive opportunity for nonprofits. Asking for payments on a monthly recurring basis is expected in the for-profit space. Shouldn't the same be true for nonprofits?

Charity:water is keenly aware that retention rates for monthly donors are north of 80 percent after the first year compared to 23 percent for new, one-time donors. Monthly donors also tend to give 42 percent more over a year.[181] The retention rates in combination with the increase in annual gift size of these donors is a potential gold mine for NPOs.

Jason was brought on board in 2017 to grow charity:water's monthly giving program, "The Spring." In a subscription product, donors can sign up to donate a specific amount automatically every month. Jason had spent decades in the startup space, leading the development of highly scalable consumer-facing software products. He was now in new territory, working with an organization whose bottom line is providing clean water rather than making money. Sure, the metrics are different, but growth was nevertheless still crucial.

"I have had experience with subscription products in the startup space, trying to get users to view emails or ads, and the question was always, 'How do you build a product for someone to sign up but then come back and engage repeatedly?'" said Jason. "When I joined charity:water, the question became, 'Can you sell a feeling? And if so, how?'"

"It's very different in the for-profit world. Charity:water does not have a product per se. We don't have a good or service that we're selling as part of our monthly subscription

---

181 "Why Recurring Giving Matters."

product. We're selling a feeling that you're contributing to something and you're doing good work by taking this monthly commitment to us. How do we make you feel good about that?" said Jason.

To do this, understanding what drives behavior is crucial at charity:water. As it relates to charity:water's monthly giving subscription product, there are two hurdles to overcome; first, how do you get donors to sign up, and second, how do you get them to stay? What feeling can you sell to convert donors?

As I navigate to charity:water's homepage, I click on a video and find myself deeply invested in what turns out to be a twenty-minute video about charity:water. I learn about their founder's journey and their amazing work to date.

After speaking with Jason about this video, I discovered I wasn't unique.

"We get people to watch a twenty-minute video, whether on our website, on Facebook, on Twitter, or any of our other marketing channels. If a potential donor makes it through the majority of this video, the likelihood that he or she joins the monthly giving program is quite high. Once you become a member of The Spring, every month, you receive an impactful story in your inbox about the difference your donation is making. We sell you the feeling and then continue to deliver that month over month."

Yes, twenty minutes. During a time where our attention spans are shorter than ever, charity:water manages to get people to sit and watch a twenty-minute video about their story. While the video is a distillation of the charity:water story, the focus is on the journey of their founder, Scott Harrison.

During the video, Scott walks me through his path from a drugged up, heavily drinking club promoter to experiencing a life-changing event and starting one of the most successful nonprofits in the United States. Charity:water has helped more than ten million people around the globe.

Scott chronicles his journey in his latest book, *Thirst: A Story of Redemption, Compassion, and a Mission to Bring Clean Water to the World*.[182]

At twenty-eight years old, Scott Harrison had it all. A top nightclub promoter in New York City, his life was an endless cycle of drugs, booze, and parties. But ten years in, desperately unhappy and morally bankrupt, he asked himself, "What would the exact opposite of my life look like?" Walking away from everything, Harrison spent the next 16 months on a hospital ship in West Africa and discovered his true calling. In 2006, with no money and less than no experience, Harrison founded Charity: Water. Today, his organization has raised over $388 million to bring clean drinking water to more than 10 million people around the globe.

When I became a donor, I knew my money was going to support charity:water, but in a way, after watching the video, I felt as if I was giving money to support my own dream—a dream to follow in Scott's footsteps. As you watch the video, you cannot help but feel moved to create your own adventure. Just as Scott is the hero of his journey, you can become the hero of yours. If he can accomplish great things after all he has been through, why can't I?

Dissect this twenty-minute video and guess what you'll find? It follows Joseph Campbell's hero's journey to a tee. Charity:water moves you to give not because they convince you through statistics and numbers that illustrate the magnitude of the problem but because they move you emotionally

---

182 Scott Harrison and Lisa Sweetingham, Thirst: A Story of Redemption, Compassion, and a Mission to Bring Clean Water to the World."

through the power of a structured narrative. They take you on a journey that connects with you at your core and then ask if you want to be a part of something bigger than yourself. After all, who wouldn't want to be?

Storytelling is a powerful way to communicate the value of a product and can be leveraged not only in marketing but also in onboarding. Furthermore, determining the "hero" of your user journey can help reframe your approach. Framing the user as the "hero" of their own journey is Pain Squad's secret sauce.

By making children the hero of their own journey, Pain Squad helps kids record their pain into their pain journals so doctors can diagnose them better. The app was developed by the iOUCH research team at The Hospital for Sick Children to help kids with cancer track their pain. Pain Squad pretends the child is in the secret police force and is tasked to hunt down pain.[183]

After downloading the app, a screen appears: "PAIN SQUAD—SPECIAL POLICE UNIT." The design looks like it is straight out of a detective movie as a police officer appears on the screen, "Hey, rookie, welcome to pain squad. It's really great that you're here. We need all the help we can get."

Children are no longer filling out a pain journal. Rather they are playing a game, which puts them at the center of the story giving doctors access to the critical information they need.

---

183 Yu-kai Chou, "Gamification to improve our world: Yu-kai Chou at TEDx-Lausanne."

All types of companies can help users achieve their goals by making them the hero of their own journey. Stories can spark a movement, inspire change, and move people to action. Throughout history, narratives have transcended time and captured us in ways that statistics and numbers cannot. As you imagine ways to engage users, remember the hero's journey. Be conscious of the journey you're asking your donors or users to embark on and remember who the hero is.

PART V:
THE FUTURE OF BEHAVIORAL SCIENCE

CHAPTER 17:

THE FUTURE OF BEHAVIORAL SCIENCE

"Behavioral science grew exponentially in the 2010s and now increasingly has the potential to design the fabric on which human lives are played out."

~IMAGINING THE NEXT DECADE
OF BEHAVIORAL SCIENCE.[184]

It's an exciting time to shape the future of behavioral science. We are in the early stages of learning the real impact of behavioral science and how applying it can help us make better decisions. With each passing year, new research comes to light, providing practitioners with new approaches and ideas to test. Below, I've assembled my thoughts about where the field is heading. These thoughts are rooted in data, experience, and a healthy dose of pure Nate speculation.

---

184 Evan Nesterak, "Imagining the Next Decade of Behavioral Science."

THE BEHAVIORAL SCIENTIST JOB GROWTH

"My hypothesis is that the 2020s is the decade for behavioral science. Jobs, industries, mandate, budget, talent, training, conversation, coverage—there's steady growth, year over year. Ten years ago, could you have ever imagined the role of a Chief Behavioral Officer in an organization? Not a chance. Today, it's a distinct competitive advantage. Even the Fortune 100s are all aboard the behavior train."

~ NICK HOBSON, FOUNDER AND CHIEF BEHAVIORAL SCIENTIST AT THE BEHAVIORIST.

As behavioral science continues its way out of academia and into the applied side to help solve everyday challenges, individuals and companies are starting to understand the power of behavioral science. They'll need the talent to help them integrate this approach into their companies, and with this comes the demand for jobs in this domain. This will become a competitive edge and companies will staff up accordingly.

DATA SCIENTIST + BEHAVIORAL SCIENTIST DREAM TEAM

Behavioral science in conjunction with data science will unlock massive opportunities. Data science, specifically machine learning, provides us the ability to make predictions based on historical data, the perfect complement to behavioral science.

As data science becomes widely adopted, companies will ask themselves, "Now that we have the data and we can use it to predict what our users will do, how do we get them to do it?"

Data science is the Yin to the Yang of behavioral science. Data science can predict what users will do, and behavioral science can nudge people to make those decisions, which is why I see a massive opportunity at the intersection of the two fields.

Imagine you have an app that helps individuals eat healthier. Your data science team discovers that male users between the ages of twenty and twenty-five in the US have a 92 percent likelihood of dropping off the platform between day ten and day twelve. Knowing this, on the ninth day, you integrate a nudge to decrease user churn. The typical approach would be to create a notification to keep users engaged, such as, "Tomorrow is day ten. Don't cancel now!"

Behavioral science flips this on its head. You now understand what type of theories to leverage as part of the onboarding process to mitigate churn. Would incorporating the endowment effect during the onboarding process help reduce this issue? What about asking users to set a specific, attainable goal to stay with the platform for at least two weeks? Or maybe place the user into a cohort on the fifth day to establish a social norm and keep them on track. Or, on the eighth day, send a text reminding them of their future self, and how they aspire to reach that person. The possibilities are endless.

WHY DIGITAL

Digital is a perfect medium for deploying and measuring the impact of behavioral science for several reasons. When implementing an intervention in a physical environment, many limitations exist that are not present in a virtual environment.

When conducting a study, we need access to research participants, the ability to randomize, the ability to implement an intervention while holding all else constant, and the ability to collect rich data on the back end.

With digital, we can run experiments with a large sample size quickly. Whether it's on an existing app or website that has significant traffic or paying participants to complete a survey, digital platforms make experimentation relatively simple.

Randomization is turnkey, as technology can handle the hard work for you. Tools such as Google Optimize allow us to easily create two variations of landing pages and randomly show users one of the two versions.

Sophisticated tools make it simple to collect the data on the backend. These tools not only allow us to collect the end data points but also provide insight into how users are navigating through the entire experiment.

Personalized to each user, digital delivers a rich, dynamic experience. Referring to the AARP example, where the app shows an older version of you, this is only possible through a digital medium. In the case where the Noom experience changes dynamically based on your inputs, if this were a paper form, it would be impossible to customize the registration process for each new user.

WHERE WILL BEHAVIORAL SCIENTISTS SPECIALIZE?

As the field of behavioral science grows, I have put a lot of thought into how we'll see specializations within the field. I have a few ideas, some of which will probably hold up against the test of time and some that won't.

BY THEORY

In the past decade, the role of data scientists within companies has seen tremendous growth. With this, data scientists are now specializing in specific industries and types of data science applications, whether it is deep learning, image recognition, or natural language processing. We may see the same structure for behavioral scientists as the field grows.

Perhaps this structure will be similar to how we diagnose and treat a sickness or injury. First, you see your primary care doctor, who evaluates you and identifies what the issue may be, and then they refer you to a specialist.

Will the future of behavioral science consist of a lead scientist who serves as the "primary care doctor?" Maybe this person will be the first line of defense. They manage the initial problem and then bring in or refer the challenge to the specialists within the field based on their findings.

I am curious if we'll see behavioral scientists specialize in a specific practice area such as social norms, commitment devices, incentives, etc. While this makes sense, theoretically, I am not sure if it does in practice, given the overlap between various theories.

BY INDUSTRY

We may see specialization by industry, for example, in consumer health, finance, or education. While this does have benefits, it can also hinder the progress of the field as a whole. At Creative Science, we say that interventions "aren't industry-specific; they are human-specific."

We see consistencies in the way humans make decisions across different industries. When contemplating how much one should save for retirement, some of the psychological hurdles one faces are the same psychological hurdles one would face when choosing a health plan.

If there are learnings to be translated across industries, having behavioral scientists who specialize in one sector could hinder progress rather than promote it.

BY COMPANY FUNCTION

The application of the knowledge in this book extends beyond digital to organizational change, marketing, communications, etc. Will we see behavioral scientists who specialize in core company functions?

BY ALL THREE

Maybe some behavioral scientists will specialize at the intersection of all three—by company function, industry, and theory. Mind blown.

ACADEMIA AND THE APPLIED SIDE COLLIDE

As noted earlier in this book, Matt Wallaert believes the academic understanding of what drives behavior precedes the implementation by about ten to fifteen years. The opportunity to bridge the gap between academia and the applied is ripe for collaboration.

As "Imagining the Next Decade of Behavioral Science" notes, "In recent years behavioral insights have captured the attention of governments, business leaders, and academics alike, yet the business community has done little to collaborate with others."[185]

Practitioners must understand how to rigorously test and apply the academic literature, and academics must

---

185 Evan Nesterak, "Imagining the Next Decade of Behavioral Science."

collaborate with practitioners to take their research out of the lab and into a real-world setting.

GETTING STARTED

"What constitutes a good behavioral scientist? What skills do they have? What similarities do they share? What outputs constitute success and prestige? Do publications, funding, or impact matter most? Do they hold any official accreditation or acknowledgment from a larger organizational entity? Does any of the above matter? Does all of it matter?"

~THE NEXT DECADE OF BEHAVIORAL SCIENCE.[186]

While I lay out several fundamental theories and approaches in this book to integrate behavioral science into product design, I assure you I have only scratched the surface. From my work, the challenge lies in bridging the gap between theory and practice. Understanding the academic literature takes time, but the real challenge is grasping cognitive biases and imagining how to integrate them into your product in a way that replicates the effect.

The field requires a creative individual who can think abstractly but simultaneously concretely to connect dots that may not seem related. This person understands how to dream up new applications of an approach, shaping and molding an idea to fit a new use case. Furthermore, this person has a solid grasp of how to leverage technology to ideate, implement, and test their approaches.

---

186 Ibid.

If you want to learn, my most significant piece of advice is to become someone's apprentice.

Learn under someone and get your hands dirty. Learn how to integrate behavioral science by, well, integrating behavioral science. An understanding of the academic literature is critical, but most studies will not fit neatly into a challenge you are facing. You have to slice and dice several existing research studies to create a new solution and then test and iterate that solution until you land on something that works.

The story in my book about Danvers and Talented and how he saw success within the apprenticeship model holds here. Start by grasping the academic literature but put your skills to the test before you are ready. Learn by getting your hands dirty and making mistakes. This will force you to think through problems, ideate potential behavioral solutions, and become accustomed to testing them.

Part of the ability to do behavioral science well comes from experience—from being exposed to vast amounts of academic literature and attempting to integrate behavioral science yourself. Over time, you'll build up your knowledge bank, and you'll begin to see patterns and intuitively know which approaches are likely to work in which scenarios.

You'll learn by taking theories and putting them into practice. You'll see where your assumptions break down and where they start to work and then hypothesize why and fine-tune it.

Learning to integrate behavioral science cannot be done overnight. To learn it well, you must invest long term, but I can assure you, if you put in the effort, it will pay dividends down the road, even when you account for those dividends being hyperbolically discounted.

CHAPTER 18:

INTEGRATING A BEHAVIORAL-FIRST APPROACH

Below are high-level steps to implement a behavioral-first approach. Disclaimer: Listed below is a watered-down, simplified version of the process. If I were to detail every step, it would be another book, but hopefully this will provide you with a starting point. It does not go into detail about best practices for running randomized controlled trials and determining statistical significance, but you can find this information online through a quick Google search.

Hopefully, you are excited about a number of the ideas you've read about in this book, and you may want to start implementing them right away, great! However, it is crucial to first focus on the behavior you're looking to change, not the solution you want to implement.

As Julie O'Brien notes, "There's this tendency to get excited about the solution and then think, 'What can we do with the solution?' We're working our way backward."

EXAMPLE—A SAVINGS APP

Imagine you have an app asking users to opt into a monthly savings plan. This is the example we'll use to outline the process at a high level. Please note, the actual process is more robust than this, but this provides a high-level overview.

GENERATE A PROBLEM STATEMENT

Create a problem statement and make it clear what you are trying to solve.

Example:
To increase the opt-in rates of new users to a recurring monthly savings plan, with a target conversion rate of 46 percent.

COLLECT THE SAY DATA

Also commonly referred to as qualitative data, collect SAY data. While this may not be the most reliable data, it is important to collect SAY data to understand your users' pain points. Do this through surveys, focus groups, and interviews. Ask users what they're thinking, feeling, seeing, and hearing. This information provides insight and a place to start.

Example:
"I don't have enough money to be able to save every month."
"I don't want to commit every month to saving."

COLLECT THE DO DATA

Once you have the SAY data, gather any DO data, known as quantitative data. Collect information about your users such as time spent on the app, bounce rate, etc. from analytics and tracking tools.

Example:

- *78 percent of users drop out of the process when they're asked to sign up for a monthly recurring savings plan.*
- *96 percent retention rates, users don't typically cancel their plan once they've signed up.*

COMPARE THE SAY VS. DO

Do the SAY data and the DO data match up? Based on what users are telling you, is that what they are doing? In this example, users said they don't want to commit every month to saving, but the DO data shows otherwise. Once they opt into the plan, they typically don't cancel. This is a key insight. Your goal then should be to figure out how to increase the likelihood they'll opt into the plan, knowing once they sign up, they don't cancel.

IDENTIFY POTENTIAL BEHAVIORAL DRIVERS

Once you've collected all the SAY data and DO data, the next step is to map these to their underlying behavioral drivers. Dig into the academic literature and come up with ideas as to what could be driving the behavior. Similar to a medical diagnosis, the SAY data is what the patient is telling the doctor, but our job is to diagnose what is causing the patient's pain. Map the SAY and DO data to potential behavioral drivers.

Example:

- *Loss Aversion—users psychologically weigh losses twice as great as an equal gain, so they are reluctant to part with their money.*
- *Present Bias—users have a hard time imagining how their future selves will benefit from saving money today, so they may be reluctant to save money for their future self.*

IDENTIFY POTENTIAL BEHAVIORAL SOLUTIONS

Now that you understand the behavioral drivers, determine which behavioral solutions to implement to offset those drivers. Dig into the academic literature and look for studies that address the drivers you're wanting to offset.

This research could be industry-specific, but it may not be. It is not uncommon to find studies in a different domain with similar underlying behaviors. It could take combining three or four different studies to come up with a behavioral solution.

Example:
- *Loss Aversion → Hyperbolic Discounting—Given that users tend to discount the value of a future option, the idea of savings in the future is not as painful as saving today. Incorporate the concept of Hyperbolic Discounting by asking users to save money at a later date, therefore discounting the "pain" a user feels when saving money.*
- *Present Bias → Mitigate Present Bias—Given that users heavily overweigh their present situation compared to the future situation, attempt to close the psychological distance between their current selves and future selves.*

CREATE INTERVENTIONS

Convert the behavioral solutions into interventions, translating an abstract concept into a something tangible that you can test.

Example:
- *Hyperbolic Discount Intervention → Leverage Hyperbolic Discounting by asking a user if they would like to commit to opting into a monthly recurring savings plan thirty days*

from today because psychologically, it is easier to commit to saving money in the future rather than today.
- *Future Self Intervention → Leverage Mitigating Present Bias by bringing their future self closer to their current self by asking them to describe what they think their life will be like in five years. This should make their future self more salient and, therefore, create more empathy for their future self.*

TEST INTERVENTIONS

Once you've developed the interventions, test the approaches. Don't aim for perfection. Seek to understand which behavioral-first method has promise and then iterate. To test your intervention, create variations of a landing where the images and copy reflect the various interventions you've designed. Be sure to randomize your tests between a control (the original landing page) and the modified landing pages (treatment conditions) based on your interventions. An excellent tool for this is Google Optimize; it is free and allows the creation of multiple variations of a web page. With this tool, website visitors will randomly see the various versions of the webpage you created.

Be careful to modify only the same sections across all conditions. This allows you to compare apples to apples. If, for instance, on one page, you move the button to a different place on the page and that page performs well, you cannot determine whether the improvement is due to your intervention or to the new position of the button.

Understand how to measure success. In this example, if you have a button to "sign up," measure the number of people who click "sign up" based on the version of the page they see. If the "asking users to sign up for a savings plan in thirty days" version drove the highest number of clicks, you can infer (if there is statistical significance) that this approach is worth iterating on.

RESOURCES
Below are some resources we use for research, testing, tracking, and implementation.

SURVEY TOOLS
- Amazon mTurk (www.mturk.com)
- Survey Monkey (www.surveymonkey.com)
- Qualtrics (www.qualtrics.com)

SPLIT TESTING AND ANALYTICS
- Google Analytics (analytics.google.com)
- Google Optimize (https://optimize.google.com/)
- Hotjar (www.hotjar.com)
- Mailchimp (www.mailchimp.com)
- Mixpanel (www.mixpanel.com/)
- Amplitude (www.amplitude.com)
- Segment (www.segment.com)

ACADEMIC RESOURCES
- Google Scholar (https://scholar.google.com/)
- The Center for Advanced Hindsight (https://advanced-hindsight.com/blog/7-best-resources-keeping-behavioral-economics-research/)
- BehavioralEconomics.com (https://www.behavioraleconomics.com/resources/)
- The Behavioral Scientist (https://behavioralscientist.org/)
- The Decision Lab (https://thedecisionlab.com/)

ACKNOWLEDGMENTS

It started with a message from Eric Koester asking if I would like to write a book. When an interesting opportunity presents itself, I default to yes and go along for the ride, and boy am I glad I did.

To Eric Koester, Brian Bies and the entire New Degree Press team for guiding me on this journey that has turned into an experience of a lifetime.

To my wonderful parents, Claudia and Richard Andorsky who saw the entrepreneurial spark in me at a young age and provided an environment from which it could thrive. I have become the person I am today because of your unconditional love and support. I love you both very much.

To my sister Lilly, brother Daniel, sister-in-law Sivi and my nephew Ezra. Thank you for always being by my side.

To my business partners Josh Behshad and Will Grana, it's been a wild ride thus far but we've stuck by each other through thick and thin. You put your faith and confidence in me to lead Creative Science and I could not be more thankful to have the two of you by my side.

To Heather Graci, Creative Science's Behavioral Econ Specialist who provided invaluable feedback, did a bunch of the heavy research and was instrumental in ensuring that everything in the book was correctly cited and edited. Thank you.

To the entire Creative Science Team, thank you for your support!

To all of those who I interviewed and provide insightful feedback and stories through this book:

Julie O'Brien	Nick Fritz
Tim Ogilvie	Nir Eyal
Brantley Boyett	Jason Kermadias
Barry Fishman	Danvers Fluery

To all of those who were early supporters of my book:

Sofi Hersher	Eric Fox
Matthew Kostinas	Nicky Sampogna
Kevin Meehan	Brendan Boerbaitz
Eric London	Mark R. Miller
Suzanne Sherman	Jesse Rose
Sam Andorsky and Rachel Siegal	Travis Neuscheler and Jenny Hollrah
Jared Gold	Max Greenblum
Josh Goodman	Tyler Hartman
Lindsey Oken	Tucker Wannamaker
Uncle Tom and Aunt Renee	Dionisios "Dio" Favatas
Harry Oken, M.D.	Alex Byers
Alex Baren	Charlie Weisman
Scott Shepard	Brad Sherman
Mike Waterman	Alex Lang
Nancy Roman	Nick Bulka
Jodi Tirengel	Tom McDougall
Audrey L. Henson	Zack Garber
Marc Troiano	Dave Briggs

Ben Winneg
Michelle Montpetit
"Danner Banks
Jim Wall
Diego Mariscal
Nancy Murphy
Henry G. Klein, Esq.
Jeffrey I. Finkelstein
Julie Veilleux
Ann and Michael Andorsky
Robert Kinsler
David Williams
Rashard J. Mendenhall
Ariel   Kahan
Allen Gannett
Neil Gallaiford
Kenneth O'Brien
Jeff Girardi
Blake Band
Zvi Band
Lisa Roberts Proffitt

Kiersten Roesemann
Trina Histon, PhD
Tyler Fishbone
Jeff Rum
The Hersher family
Dan Razulis
Terry Girardi
Johnny Bailey
Tyler Godoff
Kevin Conroy
Rob Chilton
Charo Bishop
John S. Prather
Tim Hurt
Courtney Cantor
Jesse and Rachel Rose
Steve and Colby Sciuto
Michael Celone
Cristina Roman
John and Maria Galmiche

APPENDIX + FOOTNOTES

CHAPTER 1: THE NEXT PRODUCT REVOLUTION WILL BE PSYCHOLOGICAL

Ariely, Dan. "All About Dan." Dan Ariely. Accessed on March 11, 2020.
http://danariely.com/all-about-dan/.

Ariely, Dan. "Designing for Trust." Filmed April 2019 in Porto, Portugal. TEDxPorto.
https://www.ted.com/talks/dan_ariely_designing_for_trust?language=en.

Bliss, Jeanne. "Lemonade Insurance: Powering Rapid Growth Through Radical Transparency and Technology." The Green Grid. March 12, 2019.
https://www.thegreengrid.org/en/newsroom/blog/lemonade-insurance-powering-rapid-growth-through-radical-transparency-and-technology.

Brogaard, Berit. "Split Brains." Psychology Today. November 6, 2012.
https://www.psychologytoday.com/us/blog/the-superhuman-mind/201211/split-brains.

Harris, Ainsley. "Lemonade Is Using Behavioral Science to Onboard Customers and Keep Them Honest." Fast Company. March 17, 2017.

https://www.fastcompany.com/3068506/lemonade-is-using-behavioral-science-to-onboard-customers-and-keep-them-honest.

"Internet used by 3.2 billion people in 2015." BBC. May 26, 2015. https://www.bbc.com/news/technology-32884867.

Lemonade Insurance Company. "Lemonade: Forget Everything You Know about Insurance." Accessed on February 11, 2020. https://www.lemonade.com/.

Marvin, Rob. "Tech Addiction by the Numbers: How Much Time We Spend Online." PCMag.com. June 11, 2018.

https://www.pcmag.com/news/tech-addiction-by-the-numbers-how-much-time-we-spend-online.

Nesterak, Evan. "Imagining the Next Decade of Behavioral Science." Behavioral Scientist. January 20, 2020.

https://behavioralscientist.org/imagining-the-next-decade-future-of-behavioral-science/.

Puiu, Tibi. "Your smartphone is millions of times more powerful than all of NASA's combined computing in 1969." ZME Science, last modified February 15, 2019.

https://www.zmescience.com/research/technology/smartphone-power-compared-to-apollo-432/.

Simler, Kevin, and Robin Hanson. The Elephant in the Brain: Hidden Motives in Everyday Life. Oxford University Press, 2017.

Sutherland, Rory. "The Next Revolution Will Be Psychological, Not Technological." FFWD Advertising & Marketing Week Keynote, 2013.
https://www.youtube.com/watch?v=jEVCFS3YEpk.

Sutherland, Rory. "Perspective Is Everything." Filmed December 2011 in Athens, Greece. TEDxAthens.

https://www.ted.com/talks/rory_sutherland_perspective_is_everything?language=en.

Thaler, Richard H., and Cass R. Sunstein. Nudge: Improving Decisions about Health, Wealth, and Happiness. New York: Penguin Books, 2008.

Volz, Lukas J., and Michael S. Gazzaniga. "Interaction in isolation: 50 years of insights from split-brain research." Brain 140, no. 7 (June 2017): 2051 2060. https://doi.org/10.1093/brain/awx139.

Zaltman, Gerald. How Customers Think: Essential Insights into the Mind of the Market. Harvard Business Press, 2003.

CHAPTER 2: HUMANS ARE COMPLICATED

Kahneman, Daniel. Thinking, Fast and Slow. Macmillan, 2011.

Mullainathan, Sendhil and Richard H. Thaler. "Behavioral Economics." The Library of Economics and Liberty. https://www.econlib.org/library/Enc/BehavioralEconomics.html.

Parrish, Shane and Daniel Kahneman. "Daniel Kahneman: Putting Your Intuition on Ice." In The Knowledge Project. https://fs.blog/daniel-kahneman/.

Tversky, Amos, and Daniel Kahneman. "Judgment under uncertainty: Heuristics and biases." Science 185, no. 4157 (1974): 1124-1131.

Tversky, Amos, and Daniel Kahneman. "Prospect theory: An analysis of decision under risk." Econometrica 47, no. 2 (1979): 263-291.

Vedantam, Shankar, Rhaina Cohen, Kara McGuirk-Allison, Parth Shah, Tara Boyle, and Daniel Kahneman. "Daniel

Kahneman On Misery, Memory, And Our Understanding Of The Mind." March 12, 2018. In Hidden Brain. Podcast, https://www.npr.org/2018/03/12/592986190/daniel-kahneman-on-misery-memory-and-our-understanding-of-the-mind.

CHAPTER 3: WHY WE FAIL TO MEET OUR FUTURE SELVES

Franklin Templeton Investments. "Present Bias—Investor Behavior." YouTube video, 2:37. June 6, 2017. https://www.youtube.com/watch?v=DqdElRAiRks.

Laibson, David. "Golden eggs and hyperbolic discounting." The Quarterly Journal of Economics 112, no. 2 (1997): 443-478.

Molouki, Sarah. "Increasing the Pull of the Future Self." The Decision Lab. Accessed on February 24, 2020. https://thedecisionlab.com/increasing-pull-future-self/.

Oscars. "Matthew McConaughey Winning Best Actor." YouTube video, 4:30. March 11, 2014. https://www.youtube.com/watch?v=wD2cVhC-63I.

O'Donoghue, Ted, and Matthew Rabin. "Doing it now or later." American Economic Review 89, no. 1 (1999): 103-124.

Pronin, Emily, Christopher Y. Olivola, and Kathleen A. Kennedy. "Doing unto future selves as you would do unto others: Psychological distance and decision making." Personality and Social Psychology Bulletin 34, no. 2 (2008): 224-236.

Pronin, Emily, and Lee Ross. "Temporal differences in trait self-ascription: when the self is seen as an other." Journal of Personality and Social Psychology 90, no. 2 (2006): 197-209.

Read, Daniel, and Barbara Van Leeuwen. "Predicting hunger: The effects of appetite and delay on choice." Organizational Behavior and Human Decision Processes 76, no. 2 (1998): 189-205.

Tabaka, Marla. "Most People Fail to Achieve Their New Year's Resolution. For Success, Choose a Word of the Year Instead." Inc. January 7, 2019.

https://www.inc.com/marla-tabaka/why-set-yourself-up-for-failure-ditch-new-years-resolution-do-this-instead.html.

CHAPTER 4: IMAGINING YOUR FUTURE SELF

"About AARP." AARP. 2020.

https://www.aarp.org/about-aarp/.

Ersner-Hershfield, Hal, G. Elliott Wimmer, and Brian Knutson. "Saving for the future self: Neural measures of future self-continuity predict temporal discounting," Social Cognitive and Affective Neuroscience 4, no. 1 (2009): 85-92. "FaceApp." FaceApp. 2020.

https://faceapp.com/app.

Hagan, Jean. "Survey Finds Majority of Americans Don't Think about the Future." Institute for the Future. April 13, 2017.

http://www.iftf.org/future-now/article-detail/survey-finds-majority-of-americans-dont-think-about-the-future/

Hershfield, Hal E. "The self over time." Current Opinion in Psychology 26 (2019): 72-75.

Hershfield, Hal E., Daniel G. Goldstein, William F. Sharpe, Jesse Fox, Leo Yeykelis, Laura L. Carstensen, and Jeremy N. Bailenson. "Increasing saving behavior through age-progressed renderings of the future self." Journal of Marketing Research 48, no. SPL (2011): S23-S37.

Hopkins, Jamie. "How to get investors to save more for retirement? Perhaps by saying hello to their future self." CNBC. June 20, 2019.

https://www.cnbc.com/2019/06/19/save-more-for-retirement-by-saying-hello-to-your-future-self.html.

Molouki, Sarah. "Increasing the Pull of the Future Self." The Decision Lab. Accessed on February 24, 2020. https://thedecisionlab.com/increasing-pull-future-self/.

CHAPTER 5: DESIRE TO ACHIEVE

Andorsky, Nate. "Why We're Never Satisfied—It's All in the Wiring." Medium. August 31, 2017. https://medium.com/@NateAndorsky/why-were-never-satisfied-it-s-all-in-the-wiring-875db06ba335

Carroll, Chrissy. "What Is Weight Watchers?" Verywell Fit. June 28, 2019. https://www.verywellfit.com/weight-watchers-overview-4691074.

Cherry, Kendra. "B.F. Skinner Biography: One Leader of Behaviorism." Verywell Mind. Last updated June 19, 2019. https://www.verywellmind.com/b-f-skinner-biography-1904-1990-2795543.

Combs, T. Dalton, and Ramsay A. Brown. Digital Behavioral Design. Venice Beach, CA: Boundless Mind, 2018.

Deci, Edward L., Richard Koestner, and Richard M. Ryan. "A meta-analytic review of experiments examining the effects of extrinsic rewards on intrinsic motivation." Psychological Bulletin 125, no. 6 (1999): 627-668.

Eskreis-Winkler, Lauren, Katherine L. Milkman, Dena M. Gromet, and Angela L. Duckworth. "A large-scale field experiment shows giving advice improves academic outcomes for the advisor." Proceedings of the National Academy of Sciences 116, no. 30 (2019): 14808-14810.

Eyal, Nir. Hooked: How to Build Habit-Forming Products. Penguin, 2014.

"Everything you need to know about FitPoints." WW (Weight Watchers): Weight Watchers Reimagined. 2020. https://www.weightwatchers.com/us/how-it-works/fitpoints.

Ferster, Charles B., and Burrhus Frederic Skinner. Schedules of Reinforcement. (1957).

Hamari, Juho. "Do badges increase user activity? A field experiment on the effects of gamification." Computers in Human Behavior 71 (2017): 469-478.

Hamill, Laura and Toni Best. "Watch Webinar on Demand: The Power of Intrinsic Motivation." Webinar, Limeade, October 25, 2017. https://www.limeade.com/en/2017/10/watch-webinar-on-demand-the-power-of-intrinsic-motivation/.

Lepper, Mark R., David Greene, and Richard E. Nisbett. "Undermining children's intrinsic interest with extrinsic reward: A test of the 'overjustification' hypothesis." Journal of Personality and Social Psychology 28, no. 1 (1973): 129-137.

McLeod, Saul. "Skinner—Operant Conditioning." Simply Psychology. January 21, 2018. https://www.simplypsychology.org/operant-conditioning.html.

Pink, Daniel H. Drive: The Surprising Truth about What Motivates Us. Penguin, 2011.

Pink, Dan. "The puzzle of motivation." Filmed July 2009 in Oxford, UK. TEDGlobal 2009. https://www.ted.com/talks/dan_pink_the_puzzle_of_motivation.

Sapolsky, Robert M. Behave: The Biology of Humans at Our Best and Worst. Penguin, 2017.

Skinner, Burrhus Frederic. "Superstition in the pigeon." Journal of Experimental Psychology 38, no. 2 (1948): 168.

"Student Success Guide: Extrinsic vs. Intrinsic Motivation." Excelsior College. 2020. https://guide.excelsior.edu/goals-motivation-and-attitude/motivation/extrinsic-v-intrinsic-motivation/.

Wikipedia. "Wikipedia:Statistics." Last updated February 17, 2020. https://en.wikipedia.org/wiki/Wikipedia:Statistics.

CHAPTER 6: BRIDGING THE GAP BETWEEN INTENTION AND ACTION

Ariely, Dan, and Klaus Wertenbroch. "Procrastination, deadlines, and performance: Self-control by precommitment." Psychological Science 13, no. 3 (2002): 219-224.

Dubner, Stephen J. and Steven D. Levitt. "The Stomach-Surgery Conundrum." The New York Times. November 18, 2007. https://www.nytimes.com/2007/11/18/magazine/18wwln-freakonomics-t.html?_r=1.

Giné, Xavier, Dean Karlan, and Jonathan Zinman. "Put your money where your butt is: a commitment contract for smoking cessation." American Economic Journal: Applied Economics 2, no. 4 (2010): 213-35.

Goldstein, Dan. "The battle between your present and future self." Filmed November 2011 in New York, New York. TEDSalon NY2011. https://www.ted.com/talks/daniel_goldstein_the_battle_between_your_present_and_future_self?language=en.

Johnson, Randel K. "Winning with Wellness." US Chamber of Commerce. April 7, 2016. uschamber.com/sites/default/files/022436_labr_wellness_report_opt.pdf.

Locke, Edwin A., and Gary P. Latham. A Theory of Goal Setting & Task Performance. Prentice-Hall, Inc, 1990.

Pychyl, Timothy A. "Closing the Intention-Action Gap." Psychology Today. March 11, 2009. https://www.psychologytoday.com/us/blog/dont-delay/200903/closing-the-intention-action-gap.

Rogers, Todd, Katherine L. Milkman, and Kevin G. Volpp. "Commitment devices: using initiatives to change behavior." JaMa 311, no. 20 (2014): 2065-2066.

"Tips From Former Smokers: All Groups (General Public)." Center for Disease Control and Prevention. Last updated February 15, 2019. https://www.cdc.gov/tobacco/campaign/tips/groups/general-public.html.

Trower, Matt, Catherine J. Berman, and Jamie Foehl. "B.E. For Dogs: Goal Gradient." Center for Advanced Hindsight. December 13, 2017. https://advanced-hindsight.com/blog/b-e-for-dogs-goal-gradient/.

CHAPTER 7: DON'T BREAK THE CHAIN

Ahearn, Amy. "Moving From 5% to 85% Completion Rates for Online Courses." EdSurge. June 6, 2019. https://www.edsurge.com/news/2019-06-06-moving-from-5-to-85-completion-rates-for-online-courses

Barasz, Kate, Leslie K. John, Elizabeth A. Keenan, and Michael I. Norton. "Pseudo-set framing." Journal of Experimental Psychology: General 146, no. 10 (2017): 1460.

"Don't Break the Chain—Jerry Seinfeld's Method for Creative Success." The Writer's Store. Accessed on February 19, 2020.

https://www.writersstore.com/dont-break-the-chain-jerry-seinfeld/.

Duolingo. "The story behind Duolingo's mission – Luis von Ahn, CEO." YouTube video, 1:16. July 20, 2017. https://www.youtube.com/watch?v=P_1PdQszBc8.

Gilovich, Thomas, Robert Vallone, and Amos Tversky. "The hot hand in basketball: On the misperception of random sequences." Cognitive Psychology 17, no. 3 (1985): 295-314.

Huynh, Duy, and Hiroyuki Iida. "An analysis of winning streak's effects in language course of "Duolingo." Asia-Pacific Journal of Information Technology and Multimedia 6, no. 2 (2017).

"Jerry Seinfeld Biography." Biography.com. A&E Networks Television. September 5, 2019. https://www.biography.com/performer/jerry-seinfeld.

Johnny Carson. "Jerry Seinfeld's First Appearance on Johnny Carson's Tonight Show." YouTube video, 1:31. April 2, 2011. https://www.youtube.com/watch?v=bCS0h3qLfkw.

Kron, Michaela. "The United States of Languages: An analysis of Duolingo usage state-by-state." Duolingo. October 12, 2017. https://making.duolingo.com/the-united-states-of-languages-an-analysis-of-duolingo-usage-state-by-state.

Madigan, Jamie. "Hot Hand Fallacy and Kill Streaks in Modern Warfare 2." The Psychology of Video Games. December 26, 2009. https://www.psychologyofgames.com/2009/12/hot-hand-fallacy-and-kill-streaks-in-modern-warfare-2/.

Nesterak, Evan. "Imagining the Next Decade of Behavioral Science." Behavioral Scientist. January 20, 2020.

https://behavioralscientist.org/imagining-the-next-decade-future-of-behavioral-science/.

Poulsen, Bruce. "Being Amused by Apophenia." Psychology Today. July 31, 2012. https://www.psychologytoday.com/us/blog/reality-play/201207/being-amused-apophenia.

Smale, Will. "The man teaching 300 million people a new language." BBC News. January 27, 2020. https://www.bbc.com/news/business-51208154.

"The who, what, when and why behind online education." UTEP Connect. The University of Texas at El Paso. January, 2018. https://www.utep.edu/extendeduniversity/utepconnect/blog/january-2018/the-who-what-when-and-why-behind-online-education.html

"What is Gestalt?" Gestalt Institute of Cleveland. 2016. https://www.gestaltcleveland.org/what-is-gestalt.

CHAPTER 8: THE CUES WE TAKE FROM OTHERS

Cialdini, Robert B. Influence: The Psychology of Persuasion. New York: Harper Collins, 2009.

Henderson, Rob. "The Science behind Why People Follow the Crowd." Psychology Today. May 24, 2017. https://www.psychologytoday.com/us/blog/after-service/201705/the-science-behind-why-people-follow-the-crowd.

Russo, James M. Invest Like an Aardvark. First Edition Design Publishing, 2018.

Schultz, P. Wesley, Jessica M. Nolan, Robert B. Cialdini, Noah J. Goldstein, and Vladas Griskevicius. "The constructive, destructive, and reconstructive power of social norms." Psychological Science 18, no. 5 (2007): 429-434.

Simler, Kevin, and Robin Hanson. The Elephant in the Brain: Hidden Motives in Everyday Life. Oxford University Press, 2017.

University of Leeds. "Sheep in Human Clothing: Scientists Reveal Our Flock Mentality." ScienceDaily. February 16, 2008. www.sciencedaily.com/releases/2008/02/080214114517.htm.

CHAPTER 9: MANUFACTURING A SOCIAL NORM

Andorsky, Nate. "5 Behavioral Economics Theories to Keep Your Nonprofit From Getting Left Behind—Creative Science." Next After. April 8, 2019.

https://www.nextafter.com/blog/5-behavioral-economics-theories-to-keep-your-nonprofit-from-getting-left-behind-creative-science/.

Cialdini, Robert B. Influence: The Psychology of Persuasion. New York: Harper Collins, 2009.

Gough, Christina. "US Online Gaming Industry—Statistics & Facts." Statista. March 7, 2019.

statista.com/topics/1551/online-gaming/.

Halliday, Ayun. "The Power of Conformity: 1962 Episode of Candid Camera Reveals the Strange Psychology of Riding Elevators." Open Culture. November 7, 2016.

http://www.openculture.com/2016/11/the-power-of-conformity-1962-episode-of-candid-camera-reveals-the-psychology-of-riding-elevators.html.

Henderson, Rob. "The Science Behind Why People Follow the Crowd." Psychology Today. May 24, 2017.

https://www.psychologytoday.com/us/blog/after-service/201705/the-science-behind-why-people-follow-the-crowd.

"Talented." Talented Platform, Inc. 2020.

https://www.talentedapp.com/.

CHAPTER 10: SIGNALS OF TRUST

Abrahao, Bruno, Paolo Parigi, Alok Gupta, and Karen S. Cook. "Reputation offsets trust judgments based on social biases among Airbnb users." Proceedings of the National Academy of Sciences 114, no. 37 (2017): 9848-9853.

Clements, Ron, and John Musker, dir. Aladdin. 1992; Lake Buena Vista, FL: Buena Vista Home Entertainment, 2004. DVD.

Folger, Jean. "Airbnb: Advantages and Disadvantages." Investopedia. April 11, 2019. https://www.investopedia.com/articles/personal-finance/032814/pros-and-cons-using-airbnb.asp.

Gebbia, Joe. "How Airbnb designs for trust." Filmed February 2016 in Vancouver, BC, Canada. TED2016. https://www.ted.com/talks/joe_gebbia_how_Airbnb_designs_for_trust?language=en.

Hampton, Adam J., Amanda N. Fisher Boyd, and Susan Sprecher. "You're like me and I like you: Mediators of the similarity–liking link assessed before and after a getting-acquainted social interaction." Journal of Social and Personal Relationships 36, no. 7 (2019): 2221-2244.

Oreskovic, Alexei. "Airbnb was rejected by seven investors who could have had 10 percent of the company for $150,000 in 2008." Business Insider. July 12, 2015. https://www.businessinsider.com/Airbnb-was-rejected-by-seven-investors-in-2008-2015-7.

Seidman, Gwendolyn. "Why Do We Like People Who Are Similar to Us?" Psychology Today. December 18, 2018. https://www.psychologytoday.com/us/blog/close-encounters/201812/why-do-we-people-who-are-similar-us

"Similarity/Attraction Theory." Encyclopedia.com. Last updated January 21, 2020. https://www.encyclopedia.com/social-sciences/applied-and-social-sciences-magazines/similarityattraction-theory.

CHAPTER 11: NEVER OUT OF THE GAME

Goldstein, Dan. "The battle between your present and future self." Filmed November 2011 in New York, New York. TEDSalon NY 2011. https://www.ted.com/talks/daniel_goldstein_the_battle_between_your_present_and_future_self?language=en.

HelpfulDuo. "Leaderboards now on all Android devices (updated)." Duolingo. January 18, 2019. https://forum.duolingo.com/comment/30433123/Leaderboards-now-on-all-Android-devices-updated

Koschei, Jordan. "How Duolingo Designs with Psychology in Mind." Medium. May 10, 2016. https://medium.com/in-progress/how-duolingo-designs-with-psychology-in-mind-d9472a707640.

Pérez, Lizeth Joseline Fuentes, Luciano Arnaldo Romero Calla, Luis Valente, Anselmo Antunes Montenegro, and Esteban Walter Gonzalez Clua. "Dynamic Game Difficulty Balancing in Real Time Using Evolutionary Fuzzy Cognitive Maps."

In 2015 14th Brazilian Symposium on Computer Games and Digital Entertainment (SBGames), pp. 24-32. IEEE, 2015.

Simler, Kevin, and Robin Hanson. The Elephant in the Brain: Hidden Motives in Everyday Life. Oxford University Press, 2017.

CHAPTER 12: DECISIONS, DECISIONS

Humphrey, Zara. "McKayla Maroney Opens Up on Her Life as an Olympian." Pens & Patron. September 15, 2019.

https://www.pensandpatron.com/lists/mckayla-maroney/.

Iyengar, Sheena S., and Mark R. Lepper. "When choice is demotivating: Can one desire too much of a good thing?" Journal of Personality and Social Psychology 79, no. 6 (2000): 995.

Kestenbaum, David. "Everyone Goes to the Store to Get Milk. So Why's It Way in the Back?" Produced by NPR. Planet Money. August 1, 2014. Podcast. 4:27.

https://www.npr.org/2014/08/01/337034378/everyone-goes-to-the-store-to-get-milk-so-whys-it-way-in-the-back.

Santos, Laurie and Michelle Kwan. "Episode 3: A Silver Lining." Produced by Pushkin Industries. The Happiness Lab. October 1, 2019. Podcast. 40:34.

https://www.happinesslab.fm/season-1-episodes/a-silver-lining.

Schwartz, Barry. "The Paradox of Choice: Why More is Less." New York: Ecco, 2004.

Thaler, Richard H., and Cass R. Sunstein. Nudge: Improving Decisions about Health, Wealth, and Happiness. New York: Penguin Books, 2008.

Tversky, Amos, and Daniel Kahneman. "Loss aversion in riskless choice: A reference dependent model." The Quarterly Journal of Economics 106, no. 4 (1991): 1039-1061.

CHAPTER 13: IT'S NOT WHAT YOU SAY, IT'S HOW YOU SAY IT

"Boundless Business: Decision Making." Lumen Learning. Accessed on February 26, 2020.

https://courses.lumenlearning.com/boundless-business/chapter/decision-making/.

Higgins, E. Tory, Arie W. Kruglanski, and Antonio Pierro. "Regulatory mode: Locomotion and assessment as distinct orientations." Advances in Experimental Social Psychology 35 (2003): 293-344.

Savenije, Davide. "What made Opower so successful?" Utility Dive. April 4, 2014. https://www.utilitydive.com/news/what-made-opower-so-successful/247044/.

Tversky, Amos, and Daniel Kahneman. "The framing of decisions and the psychology of choice." Science 211, no. 4481 (1981): 453-458.

"Why option presentation changes our decision making." The Decision Lab. Accessed on February 26, 2020. https://thedecisionlab.com/biases/framing-effect/.

CHAPTER 14: SOMETHING TO LOSE

"Adult Obesity Facts." Centers for Disease Control and Prevention. Last updated February 27, 2020. https://www.cdc.gov/obesity/data/adult.html.

Buell, Ryan W., and Michael I. Norton. "Think Customers Hate Waiting? Not So Fast..." Harvard Business Review. May, 2011. https://hbr.org/2011/05/think-customers-hate-waiting-not-so-fast.

Caporuscio, Jessica. "Everything you need to know about the Noom diet." Medical News Today. November 25, 2019. https://www.medicalnewstoday.com/articles/327114.

Chen, James. "Sunk Cost Dilemma." Investopedia. Last updated September 8, 2019. https://www.investopedia.com/terms/s/sunk-cost-dilemma.asp.

Chin, Sang Ouk, Changwon Keum, Junghoon Woo, Jehwan Park, Hyung Jin Choi, Jeong-taek Woo, and Sang Youl Rhee. "Successful weight reduction and maintenance by using a smartphone application in those with overweight and obesity." Scientific Reports 6, no. 1 (2016): 1-8.

Kahneman, Daniel, Jack L. Knetsch, and Richard H. Thaler. "Anomalies: The endowment effect, loss aversion, and status quo bias." Journal of Economic Perspectives 5, no. 1 (1991): 193-206.

Michaelides, Andreas, Christine Raby, Meghan Wood, Kit Farr, and Tatiana Toro-Ramos. "Weight loss efficacy of a novel mobile Diabetes Prevention Program delivery platform with human coaching." BMJ Open Diabetes Research and Care 4, no. 1 (2016).

"Noom Announces Investment from Serena Ventures." Business Wire. September 26, 2019. https://www.businesswire.com/news/home/20190926005011/en/Noom-Announces-Investment-Serena-Ventures.

Norton, Michael I., Daniel Mochon, and Dan Ariely. "The IKEA effect: When labor leads to love." Journal of Consumer Psychology 22, no. 3 (2012): 453-460.

Reis, Harry T. "Similarity-attraction effect." Encyclopedia of Social Psychology (2007): 875-876.

Santos, Laurie and Michelle Kwan. "Episode 3: A Silver Lining." Produced by Pushkin Industries. The Happiness Lab. October 1, 2019. Podcast. 40:34. https://www.happinesslab.fm/season-1-episodes/a-silver-lining.

Tversky, Amos, and Daniel Kahneman. "Prospect theory: An analysis of decision under risk." Econometrica 47, no. 2 (1979): 263-291.

CHAPTER 15: THE POWER OF PEANUTS AND DEFAULTS

Berman, Kristen. "How behavioral scientists build products." Webinar, Irrational Labs, January 17, 2020.

Chiu, Alexander S., Raymond A. Jean, Jessica R. Hoag, Mollie Freedman-Weiss, James M. Healy, and Kevin Y. Pei. "Association of lowering default pill counts in electronic medical record systems with postoperative opioid prescribing." JAMA Surgery 153, no. 11 (2018): 1012-1019.

CNBC Television. "Investing app Acorns CEO hopes for an IPO one day." YouTube video, 5:03. January 28, 2019. https://www.youtube.com/watch?v=F4EdsAdVi2A.

Gazel, Sümeyra. "The Regret Aversion as an Investor Bias." International Journal of Business and Management Studies 4, no. 2 (2015): 419-424.

MacLaughlin, Steve, Chuck Longfield, and Angele Vellake. "Charitable Giving Report: How Nonprofit Fundraising Performed in 2018." Blackbaud Institute for Philanthropic Impact. February, 2019. https://institute.blackbaud.com/wp-content/uploads/2019/02/2018CharitableGivingReport.pdf.

Neal, Ryan W. "Shlomo Benartzi to chair Acorns behavioral economics committee." Investment News. September 21, 2018. https://www.investmentnews.com/shlomo-benartzi-to-chair-acorns-behavioral-economics-committee-76168.

"Opioid Overdose Crisis." National Institute on Drug Abuse. Last updated February, 2020. https://www.drugabuse.gov/drugs-abuse/opioids/opioid-overdose-crisis.

Samuelson, William, and Richard Zeckhauser. "Status quo bias in decision making." Journal of Risk and Uncertainty 1, no. 1 (1988): 7-59.

Shimizu, Kazumi, and Daisuke Udagawa. "Is human life worth peanuts? Risk attitude changes in accordance with varying stakes." PloS One 13, no. 8 (2018).

Sunstein, Cass R. "With Clean-Energy Default Rules, It's Easy Being Green." Bloomberg Businessweek. April 4, 2013. https://www.bloomberg.com/news/articles/2013-04-04/with-clean-energy-default-rules-its-easy-being-green.

Parbhoo, Omar. "I Think, Therefore I Am—Generous?" Behavioral Scientist. March 5, 2018. https://behavioralscientist.org/think-therefore-generous/.

CHAPTER 16: DRIVEN BY EMOTION

Beament, Emily. "McDonald's to ban plastic straws in all of its restaurants in UK and Ireland." The Independent. June 15, 2018. https://www.independent.co.uk/news/business/news/mcdonalds-plastic-straws-ban-uk-ireland-pollution-environment-eu-rules-a8399841.html.

Borenstein, Seth. "Science Says: Amount of straws, plastic pollution is huge." Phys.org. April 21, 2018. https://phys.org/news/2018-04-science-amount-straws-plastic-pollution.html

Campbell, Joseph. The Hero with a Thousand Faces. Vol. 17. New World Library, 2008.

Chou, Yu-kai. "Gamification to improve our world: Yu-kai Chou at TEDxLausanne." Filmed February 2014 in Lausanne, Switzerland.

"Eye Reading (Body Language)." Psychologist World. Accessed February 19, 2020. https://www.psychologistworld.com/body-language/eyes.

Fenston, Jacob. "Plastic Straws Now Officially Banned in DC" WAMU 88.5. January 2, 2019. https://wamu.org/story/19/01/02/plastic-straws-now-officially-banned-in-d-c/.

"Food Service Packaging Requirements." Seattle.gov. Accessed February 19, 2019. http://www.seattle.gov/utilities/businesses-and-key-accounts/solid-waste/food-and-yard/commercial-customers/food-packaging-requirements.

Harrison, Scott, and Lisa Sweetingham. Thirst: A Story of Redemption, Compassion, and a Mission to Bring Clean Water to the World. Currency, 2018. TEDxLausanne. https://www.youtube.com/watch?v=v5Qjuegtiyc.

"Infographic: The Science of Storytelling." One Spot. 2017. https://www.onespot.com/resources/the-science-of-storytelling-infographic/.

Jambeck, Jenna R., Roland Geyer, Chris Wilcox, Theodore R. Siegler, Miriam Perryman, Anthony Andrady, Ramani Narayan, and Kara Lavender Law.

"Plastic waste inputs from land into the ocean." Science 347, no. 6223 (2015): 768-771.

Jenni, Karen, and George Loewenstein. "Explaining the identifiable victim effect." Journal of Risk and Uncertainty 14, no. 3 (1997): 235-257.

Josephson, Brady. "The Science Behind Storytelling and How to Use the Pixar Framework." Medium. February 16, 2017.

https://blog.bradyjosephson.com/storytelling-science-and-the-pixar-framework-efde445eed94.

Kahneman, Daniel. "Maps of bounded rationality: Psychology for behavioral economics." American Economic Review 93, no. 5 (2003): 1449-1475.

Lee, Jane J. "How Did Sea Turtle Get a Straw Up Its Nose?" National Geographic. June 5, 2018.
https://www.nationalgeographic.com.au/animals/how-did-sea-turtle-get-a-straw-up-its-nose.aspx.

Ludden, David. "Your Eyes Really Are the Window to the Soul." Psychology Today. December 31, 2015.
https://www.psychologytoday.com/us/blog/talking-apes/201512/your-eyes-really-are-the-window-your-soul.

Meyer, Zlati. "Big food-service outfit banning plastic straws at more than 1,000 US eateries." USA Today. May 31, 2018.
https://www.usatoday.com/story/money/2018/05/31/plastic-straws-banned-eateries/657172002/. 768-771.

Nichols, Hannah. "Babies recognize face-like patterns before birth." Medical News Today. June 12, 2017.
https://www.medicalnewstoday.com/articles/317869#1.

Oppenheimer, Daniel M., and Christopher Y. Olivola, eds. The Science of Giving: Experimental Approaches to the Study of Charity. Psychology Press, 2011.

"Our Mission." Charity: Water. Accessed February 19, 2020. https://my.charitywater.org/about/mission.

O'Sullivan, Kevin. "The Best Writing Formula for Epic Marketing Content." Story Block. April 2, 2018.
https://www.storyblock.media/blog/heros-journey-guide-to-master-marketing.

Pink, Daniel H. To Sell Is Human: The Surprising Truth about Moving Others. Penguin, 2013.

Rochman, Bonnie. "Straws are out, lids are in: Starbucks announces environmental milestone." Starbucks Stories. July 9, 2018. https://stories.starbucks.com/stories/2018/starbucks-announces-environmental-milestone/.

Rose, Frank. "The Art of Immersion: Why Do We Tell Stories?" Wired. March 8, 2011. https://www.wired.com/2011/03/why-do-we-tell-stories/.

Sapolsky, Robert M. Behave: The Biology of Humans at Our Best and Worst. Penguin, 2017.

Trafton, Anne. "In the blink of an eye." MIT News. January 16, 2014. http://news.mit.edu/2014/in-the-blink-of-an-eye-0116.

Vedantam, Shankar, Laura Kwerel, Angus Chen, Thomas Lu, Tara Boyle, and Rhaina Cohen. "Tell Me a Story: What Narratives Reveal about the Mind." January 9, 2020. In Hidden Brain. Podcast, https://www.npr.org/2020/01/09/794683840/tell-me-a-story-what-narratives-reveal-about-the-mind.

"We Read Emotions Based on How the Eye Sees." Association for Psychological Science. February 22, 2017. https://www.psychologicalscience.org/news/releases/we-read-emotions-based-on-how-the-eye-sees.html.

"Why Recurring Giving Matters." Network for Good. Accessed February 19, 2020. https://www.networkforgood.com/lesson/why-recurring-giving-matters/.

CHAPTER 17: WHAT'S NEXT FOR BEHAVIORAL SCIENCE

Nesterak, Evan. "Imagining the Next Decade of Behavioral Science." Behavioral Scientist. January 20, 2020. https://behavioralscientist.org/imagining-the-next-decade-future-of-behavioral-science/.

Made in the USA
Monee, IL
21 June 2020